Dear Jris,
A Blessed Christmas. Thanks
for your being a fellow traveler.

Fellow Travelers

Reflections on the Seasons of the Church Year

by Terry R. Morehouse

Pastor Terry Morehouse

Kirk House Publishers
Minneapolis, Minnesota

Fellow Travelers

Reflections on the Seasons of the Church Year

Library of Congress Cataloging-in-Publication-Data

Morehouse, Terry, 1941
    Fellow travelers : reflections on the seasons of the church year / by terry Morehouse.
        p.cm.
    ISBN 1-886513-28-7 (alk. paper)
        1. Church year meditations. I Title.
BV30 .M63 2001
242'.3—dc21

                                                    2001050450

Kirk House Publishers, PO Box 390759, Minneapolis, MN 55439
Manufactured in the United States of America

Contents

Easter

Pentecost

To my wife, Joan,
my "fellow traveler" in marriage and in life,
who has been my source of greatest inspiration
and my friend.

Foreword

Finding myself a Fellow Traveler with Terry Morehouse on a journey through his ideas and stories was a gift. Terry has woven together legends, scripture and stories from his own life as we travel with him into the mysteries, pains and joys of life.

I smiled at his description of a child stalling at bedtime and went with him as he biked along a country road to a wood frame church called Faith, where he foundour awesome God. I was touched by Terry's poem picture as he reflects on the life and fading strength of his father. In "A Little Child Shall Lead Them" Terry, the pastor, discovers the personal gift of a quiet Christmas and lightly pokes fun at himself.

Terry takes us with him on our journey of life; when we're in water up to our necks, when we discover the rich blessings of friendships, when God changes a family's life as a three-year-old sings a song to the darkness, and when we're challenged to acknowledge that we have a God for the "polished" outside as well as the "inside" crawl spaces of our lives and hearts.

Fellow Traveler is a book I expect to read again and again. As Terry reminds us, we are connected as the saints of Christ, walking together, grateful that Jesus is walking with us. As we welcome all that life has to offer, we discover with him that Jesus is the beginning and the end of our restless journeys. Thanks, Terry!

The Rev. Judith Mattison
Bethlehem Lutheran Church

Introduction and Appreciation

The image of Abraham and his family beginning their journey into the vast unknown has always intrigued me. It may not be profound, nor is it new, but seeing life as a "journey" makes sense to me. Each year, each month, each day, each hour, the journey begins anew. "By faith Abraham obeyed…and he set out, not knowing where he was going." (Hebrews 11:8)

It's true that we seldom know where we are going. It's also true that we do not travel alone. There are, our "fellow travelers". And there is this One we know, this "Mystery of All That Is" who promises to travel with us.

Very early in my ministry I began to use that phrase, "fellow travelers," to begin either an article in a campus paper or a church newsletter, and for the past eight years to begin a radio broadcast that's called "Faith Alive." In this book I have selected fifty-two reflections that I have shared in these broadcasts throughout the years. For the most part they have been inspired by the scriptures of the Common Lectionary assigned to a particular Sunday in the Church Year or from some of the wonderful writings and stories that have enriched my life throughout this time. They are shared with you, the reader, in the hope that they will connect with your life as they have with mine.

My special thanks to all of those who contributed stories and poems and thoughts to this book, and they are acknowledged either in the reflection itself or the back of this book.

A very special thank you to my good friend and former secretary Molly Borgeson. She has been my diligent and tireless editor, and this couldn't have happened without her. Since each of these reflections were originally written to be spoken, her challenges were many. I'm grateful as well to Pastor

Paul Youngdahl, my colleague, my boss, and my friend for his solid support along the way. Also, a very special thanks to Kirk House Publishers, and to Leonard Flachman for his wisdom and his encouragement from the beginning to the end. To Mary Strand, my sister-in-law, for her support as well as her cover picture. For the love and encouragement of the members and friends of Mount Olivet Lutheran Church, I also say, "Thank You!" This could never have happened without you, my "fellow travelers", who have always been my greatest inspiration.

Terry R. Morehouse

Advent

Every valley shall be lifted up...
...every hill be made low.
Isaiah 40:4

A Different Kind of Coming

Scripture: Mark 13:24-25: "But in those days, after that suffering, the sun will be darkened, and the moon will not give its light, and the stars will be falling from heaven, and the powers in the heavens will be shaken."

Stir up your power and come" we pray together in our prayer for the First Sunday in Advent.

With Thanksgiving having come and gone, we come together as the people of God into the Season of Advent, the first Sunday of a brand new year in the life of our church. I would wager that when we think of Advent, we most often think the thoughts of Christmas coming. We think of a baby being born in Bethlehem, of shepherds keeping watch over their flocks by night, and of three kings coming from the east. That's the message that we're expecting to hear when we come to this season, then we must have been surprised when we heard the reading of the Gospel Lesson for this day. "In those days, after that suffering," said Jesus, "the sun will be darkened, and the moon will not give its light, and the stars will be falling from heaven, the powers in the heaven will be shaken."

This is a different kind of coming to be sure. We pray, "Stir up your power and come," but this isn't the kind of coming we were thinking about! These are the words that tell of Christ's coming again. Oftentimes they are words that send a chill within us, stirring up our sense of guilt and fear and faithless-ness, and often turning us off! We really don't want to hear about Christ's coming again nor do we want to hear about the end of the world as we know it.

We would rather hear about a little child who is born in sweetness and love.

Yet, the Scriptures barely blush to tell the news that Christ will come again, even if we stick our fingers in our ears, trying we might, not to hear.

"And he will come again to judge the living and the dead," we confess together in our Apostle's Creed, and there it is again, Sunday after Sunday.

The Scriptures remind us that we are accountable. We have been given this precious gift called time, and our time will not last forever. The promise that He will come again reminds us that each day is a gift: Christ waits to touch the world once more with his love. He does this through those that he has called to be his own, those that he has gathered together in his church. That Christ will come again is a message of hope, and a reason for dreaming of a better world, a new world that is waiting to be born. That Christ will come again is the assurance that when He comes, He comes in love and the forgiveness of the Cross. This is Good News, not bad.

That Christ will come again heightens our sense of the importance of each and every moment of our lives. Writes William Joyner:

> Each morning
>> The sun greets the earth
>> Kissing its open face
>> With life.
>
> And as it clings to the warmth,
>> Each spot of soil
>> Is seduced to believe
>> That it's bright visitor
>> Is there to stay.
>
> But in vain
>> For soon
>> As always
>> The voice of evening
>> Whispers from some darkening place,
>> "Your time is up..."

Today, just for an instant
    There is time
    To cast light and warmth
    Into the dark corners
    To salt the earth.

But who knows
    For how long?
    Whoever knows
    How much time remains
    Before the Lord of time will come

Like some teacher collecting papers,
    And say, "Friend,
    Your time is up."

Prayer: There is time today, O God, to cast light and warmth into the darkened corners and to salt the earth. Thank you for this precious gift. Help us to know that you will come again, and You come even now, in love. We pray in Jesus Name. Amen.

The Legend of St. Nicholas

Scripture: Philippians 1:9: And this is my prayer, that your love may overflow more and more with knowledge and full insight."

As Christmas edges into our lives during these Advent days, let me share with you the story of still another saint in our Christian tradition. His name was Nicholas. The special day that the church has set aside to honor him is December 6th.

Information about the good bishop is sketchy, to be sure. You'll soon discover that it's also highly legendary, yet there is much that we can learn from his model.

Nicholas was born around the year 280 C.E., in a small town in Asia Minor, which is present day Turkey. His mother had long prayed for a child. Much like Hannah in the Old Testament, she had promised God that her firstborn would be dedicated to God's services. Even as an infant, the legends tell us, Nicholas was a religious child. It is said that on holy days he would fast by refusing his mother's breasts until after sunset!

Shortly after the turn of the century, Nicholas became Bishop of Myra, where he was a kind and generous pastor. It was not an easy time to be a bishop. The church was faced with enemies from both the outside and within. When the emperor Diocletion began his ugly persecution of the Christian church, Nicholas and his people suffered. When Arius attempted to subvert the true teaching of the church, Nicholas helped to gather a council at Nicaea in 325, uniting the church against Arianism and solidifying its beliefs through the formation of the Nicene Creed, a creed that most Christians still include as a vital part of their worship.

Perhaps the most famous story of Nicholas concerns a man who lived alone with his three lovely daughters. The poor man was not able to provide a dowry for any of his girls, which meant that they would be unable to marry. Poor girls in those days were either sold into slavery or they became prostitutes, both horrible choices. To save the eldest daughter, Nicholas placed a large number of gold pieces in a small bag and tossed it through the open window. Later he did the same for the two younger women. Though he attempted to provide the gifts anonymously, the father discovered him during the third visit. Many people think that this is the origin of giving gifts at Christmas. During the middle ages, pictures of Nicholas always included three gold pouches.

Traditions surrounding St. Nicholas developed in European countries under different names. In Germany he is Wehnachtsmann, Pere Noel in France, and Father Christmas in England. In Holland he is known either as St. Nicholas or Sinta Claes from which we get our Santa Claus.

The Dutch legend is said to have begun when Nicholas traveled to Holland from Myra, dressed in his red bishop robes, riding a white horse, and accompanied by his servant Black Bart. As he rode through the streets he carried a sack full of gifts for the children—toys, oranges and coins. Wherever he saw a child he asked their parents, "Has your child been good?" If the answer was "yes," the boy or girl received a gift. If the answer was "no," Black Bart shook a stick at the children, who ran and hid behind their mother's skirts. People understood that the presents the good bishop delivered were gifts from God.

One day, as the legend goes, Nicholas and Black Bart came to a small hut where there were no windows and the doors were closed. "How shall we deliver our gifts?" Nicholas asked Bart.

Looking up at the roof, Black Bart suggested that they drop the presents through the chimney. "Splendid idea," the bishop exclaimed. The two men climbed the roof and dropped the gifts through the chimney. Miraculously, the gifts all landed in the stockings that the children had hung up to dry! Thus a new custom was born.

Few saints give inspiration to as many groups and nations as the gentle Bishop of Myra. While it's true that many of these stories are rooted in legend, there is a truth that emerges from all of them. At the heart of this message of the coming of Jesus Christ, there is a spirit of generosity and kindness. "Your love may overflow," as St. Paul puts it.

It is the same message that reaches out to you and me once again this year, urging us to look beyond our own needs, even beyond the needs of our family and friends, to touch the lives of others with kindness and a generous heart.

Prayer: Come into our hearts and our lives, Lord Jesus, making room for our love of others this year. Help us to be inspired by the saints of old, like he who was Bishop of Myra, so that our own lives will be transformed through the magic of giving. We pray in Jesus Name. Amen.

Not What You Have But Who

Scripture: Luke 1:45 "And blessed is she who believed that there would be a fulfillment of what was spoken to her by the Lord."

One of the greatest miracles of Luke's Christmas story Martin Luther would say was that Mary "believed." Mary's faith is at the heart of the message of Advent.

In 1994, two Americans answered an invitation from the Russian Department of Education to teach in Russia. They were invited to teach at many places, including a large orphanage. About 100 boys and girls, who had been abandoned and abused and left in care of a government-run program, were in the orphanage. The two Americans relate the following story in their own words:

> It was nearing the holiday season, 1994, time for our orphans to hear for the first time the traditional story of Christmas. We told them about Mary and Joseph arriving in Bethlehem. Finding no room in the inn, the couple went to a stable, where the baby Jesus was born and placed in a manger.

> Throughout the story, the children and the orphanage staff sat in amazement as they listened. Some sat on the edges of their stools, trying to grasp every word. Completing the story, we gave the children three small pieces of cardboard to make a crude manger.

> Each child was given a small paper square, cut from yellow napkins I had brought with me. No colored paper was available in the city. Following instructions, the children tore the paper and carefully laid strips in the manger for straw. Small squares of flannel, cut from a worn out nightgown an American lady was throwing away as she left Russia, were used for the baby's blanket.

A doll-like baby was cut from tan felt we had brought from the United States. The orphans were busy assembling their manger as I walked among them to see if they needed any help. All went well until I got to one table where little Misha sat. He looked to be about six years old, and had finished his project. As I looked at the little boy's manger, I was startled to see not one, but two babies in the manger. Crossing his arms in front of him and looking at this completed manger scene, the child began to repeat the story, very seriously. For such a young boy, who had only heard the Christmas story once, he related the happenings accurately—until he came to the part where Mary put the baby Jesus in the manger. Then Misha started to ad-lib. He made up his own ending to the story as he said, "And when Maria laid the baby in the manger, Jesus looked at me and asked if I had a place to stay. I told him I have no mamma and I have no papa, so I don't have any place to stay. Then Jesus told me I could stay with him. But I told him I couldn't because I didn't have any gift to give him, like everybody else did. But I wanted to stay with Jesus so much, so I thought about what I had that maybe I could use for a gift. I thought maybe if I kept him warm, that would be a good gift.

So I asked Jesus, "If I keep you warm, will that be a good enough gift?" And Jesus told me, "If you keep me warm, that will be the best gift anyone ever gave me." So I got into the manger, and then Jesus looked and at me and told me I could stay with him...for always.

As little Misha finished his story, his eyes brimmed full of tears that splashed down his little cheeks. Putting his hands over his face, his head dropped to the table and his shoulders shook as he sobbed and sobbed.

The little orphan had found someone who would never abandon him or abuse him, someone who would stay with him—for always.

Perhaps there is a lesson here, the author suggests. That it's not so much what you have in your life, but whom you have in your life that counts.

Prayer: You have come into our world, O Christ, as a child, born of Mary. Our world is often "hard as iron, cold as ice," and often turns to stone in the faces and the places of our living. Allow your love to warm us once again, O Christ. Help us to believe that You have come, for us, for always. In Jesus Name. Amen.

Surprised by Silence

Scripture: Isaiah 11:6. The wolf shall live with the lamb, the leopard shall lie down with the kid, the calf and the lion and the fatling together, and a little child shall lead them.

December days can be a little scary. "So much to do, so little time," as they say. So often we get to Christmas, and say, what happened? Those Advent days have disappeared, and we've scarcely taken time to pause, and wonder what they mean.

Several years ago now, as December dawned, I found myself thinking a lot about my upcoming surgery. It was scheduled for the first week in December, and I knew that this year my Advent days would be vastly different than they had ever been in my life. I knew, for one thing, that I wouldn't be in church at Christmas, for the first time in over thirty years of ministry. Instead, I would be resting at home, recuperating, and letting the Advent days slowly unwind without the bustle and the rush of all of those things that seemed so important.

It turned out to be a magical time for me. When the soft snows of December came falling down, all I could do was sit and watch them fall. I didn't have to shovel. I didn't have to drive anywhere. I didn't have any sermons to write, or patients to see in the hospital, or parties to attend. I could simply sit and watch the falling snow; listening to the Spirit's voice, reminding me that the world would get along quite well without me this year.

I got to know my wife again. She took some time off too, to be my personal nurse and to pamper me. I did my therapy to strengthen those muscles around my brand new hip. But basically I sat, with my crutches at my side, as the lights of Christmas began to shine around me and within me.

On Christmas Eve the family came to our house so I could stay at home. We worshipped in our living room that year, singing the beautiful carols together, listening to the Christmas story from the Gospel of Luke, and old dad even shared a Christmas story as a sermon, reminding us of earlier days.

"How silently, how silently, the wondrous gift is given," our beloved carol sings. That year I came to appreciate the wonder of the silence of Christmas, and the wonderful words of that hymn in a brand new way.

I even scratched out a poem, that I share with you now. I called it "A Christmas Hip"

> A pastor was home at Christmas.
> Confined to the walls,
> With an afghan shawl
> Around him!
>
> The need for a hip had started this trip
> At this holy time
> Of year.
>
> After thirty years of Christmas cheer,
> Delivering sermons in rapid succession
> Counseling others, and private confessions,
> He hardly had time
> For his own depression!
> And now here he sat!
>
> Could the world, should the world,
> Would the world,
> Would his family,
> Survive?
> Holy Smokes alive!
> Could he?
>
> Ah, yes! T'is true believe it!
> T'was not his demise,
> But to his surprise, the Spirit
> Came into their lives.

Like a dove from above
Came the Christ
In love
And the pastor wasn't in charge!

Prayer: We need reminding, O God, that we can easily miss your coming in the busyness of these days. Quiet us. Encourage us to take time. Help us to see how you catch our world off guard, when a little child is born. In His name we pray. Amen.

Christmas

And a little child shall lead them...

Isaiah 11:6

More Powerful Than Prisons

St. Stephen, Deacon and Martyr

Scripture: Acts 7:60 "Then he knelt down and cried out in a loud voice, "Lord do not hold this sin against them." When he had said this, he died."

Just yesterday the "Bells of Christmas" rang once more. We sang with gusto, "Joy to the World, the Lord has come!" We ushered in God's great good news that the Word had become flesh, and dwelt among us. Is there any other message that we need to hear more desperately than that?

Today the church fathers have inserted a day in our church year that seems to be completely juxtaposed to all those joyful voices that sang on Christmas. It is a day to remember Stephen, the first Christian martyr. It is a day to remember his death.

Surrounded by those who refused to hear of Jesus Christ, or to accept that he was the promised one of God, Stephen knelt down and cried in a loud voice reminiscent of Christ on the Cross. "Lord do not hold this against them." And when he had said this, our text tells us, "He died." St. Stephen, Deacon and Martyr was stoned to death for the sake of his belief.

Strange that we should be asked to face such realities so close to Christmas, you say?

Perhaps. Yet good. Good because we need to remember that Jesus Christ was born because of such realities. Good because St. Stephen's witness reminds us that Jesus Christ was born because of the blindness of men and women everywhere. They fail to see that in Him we have been given the Grace of God. Good because St. Stephen's death reminds us that God's love for us in this child, has always been, and will always be stronger than death.

Becca Stevens shares with us the story of Jane.

Jane was a prostitute and drug abuser for over 23 years. She has now become a graduate of a beauty school, and is a skillful beautician who practices her cutting and blow-drying skills on my short hair. Over the last two years, I have let her cut my hair (which used to be fairly long!) shorter and shorter. As the months have gone by, I have watched her grow as a beautician and a child of God.

I remember visiting Jane in the jail in 1996, after her 258th arrest for prostitution or possession of drugs. She couldn't believe her sobriety hadn't lasted this time. She had been sober for almost four months.

Just when she had started to breathe again, she found herself using drugs, and was arrested within a week. With her jaw squarely set as she leaned against the prison cot she said, "This time I am ready. I am ready to make a change, and ready to try and ask my family for forgiveness." The life of a captive was completely exhausting she said, and she had been abusing and abused for long enough. She had found some peace in a recovery program in the jail, and all she needed was time, prayer, and help.

The problem is that no one takes chances on women like her. After so many relapses, the promises sound empty. Captivity seems to be the only place she is sober and honest.

But there was some hope. A new recovery house for women coming out of jail had just opened. We invited Jane to be one of our first participants. The program was the result of long research into the problems of prostitution and collaboration on the part of several agencies in Nashville.

So Jane moved into the new Magdalene House and entered an intensive treatment program. For six months she struggled to try to rebuild her life. It was hard for her to accept even the gifts of freedom and hospitality that she was being offered. What did this new home and new life mean? She came home from treatment one afternoon about five months after her release and said, "I love the way the house looks with all of these Christmas decorations. Did you know that I have never celebrated Christmas before in a home? I just can't figure out what happened to me. How did I get from 23 years on the streets to living here in their beautiful home, surrounded by a community that is supporting and loving me?"

"It just feels like I dreamed this and then I woke up from a long fog and am living in the middle of it." As the tears began to roll down her cheek she said, "Do you understand? I am singing again. I have held my grand-child. I have made amends, and I have forgiven my mother and father for stuff that happened over 40 years ago."

I was at a loss for words and stood there with her, feeling my own eyes well up with tears.

I know that God's love is constant and eternal. My experience of love that afternoon with Jane, though, was more like a giant wave that swept me up in its power and reminded me of the magnitude of God's grace and compassion. Her tears that day reminded me that God's love is more powerful than the strongest prisons, and can overcome any estrangement. Jane gave me a wonderful Christmas present (that) year. She gave me the chance to experience the good news of God in Christ, and by her life has stated loudly and clearly that God's Spirit is alive and well.

When I left that November afternoon, I kept think-ing how incredible Christmas must feel for people like Jane, whose Advent had lasted for 23 years."

Prayer: For the life of St. Stephen, O God, Deacon and Martyr we give you thanks today. For his words and his death, which remind us today that your love is more powerful than the strongest of prisons. Thank you for reminding us that you gave us your Son for realities like these, and that you continue to come into our prisons, ready to release us, and to make us free. In the name of the One who came, Jesus Christ our Lord, we pray. Amen.

A Child Who Changes The World

Luke 2:34: "Then Simeon blessed them and said to his mother Mary, "This child is destined for the falling and the rising of many in Israel..."

What do you say on December the 27th when Christmas is all over? What do you say when all the expectations and the anticipations have suddenly fizzled or faded? What do you say when all the season's hype seems settled and austere? Christmas is almost surrealistic. But when it's over, all the realism of living and life, are staring us in the eye once again. It's back to life as usual on December 27th.

For the Morehouse family it was a Christmas that was peppered with surprises, not the least of which was the birth of a beautiful baby girl named Carly Marie Madigan, our third grandchild. If you thought I was obnoxious about the first two, then just you wait, you haven't heard the last of this one, that's for sure!

Tears filled my eyes as I looked at this child for the very first time. She was beautiful. She was whole. She had ten fingers, ten toes, and every part seemed to be in place, a blessing beyond all belief. I couldn't let go. I just couldn't leave the hospital room, as I held her and saw her for the very first time.

I wondered how it was a long time ago, when a mother named Mary and scared young man named Joseph gazed down at their child. I wondered what they thought as Simeon blessed him, saying these strange words, "This child is destined for the falling and rising of many in Israel..."

In Martin Bell's book *The Way of the Wolf* he has written a song that ponders these same questions:

Who could have dreamed that this little baby,
Here in the manger, crying for his momma—
Who could have dreamed that this little baby
Would change the course of the world?

Hush-a-bye, go to sleep little baby
Here in the manger, safe beside your momma.
Only the angel's who watch as you're sleeping
Know that you'll change the world.

And tonight the silent stars behold him,
Shining their brightest to try to keep from crying.
Did they guess? Or have the angels told them,
The price of changing the world?

The stars shine bright?
What do they know?
Is there a secret they keep?
O holy night. The child shivers so.
What fearful thought disturbs his sleep?

Today other mommas are holding their children.
Children who'll grow up and follow where he leads them.
God have mercy,
And comfort all the mommas
Of children who'll change the world.

**Prayer: O Lord, I'm thankful this morning for the gift of
Carly Marie and for the gift of children everywhere. With
each child born we know you share your hope. With each
one born, we can see the softness of your signature, and we
know that you are here, "Emmanuel" still with us today.
Thank you for blessing our world with Jesus, who meets us
today in the real worlds in which we live. Thank you for the
price that he was willing to pay, the cost of changing the
world. May the magic of Christmas live in all of your children, who were born to change the world. In Jesus name.
Amen.**

The Name of Jesus
New Year's Day

Scripture: Luke 2:21 "At the end of the eighth day, when the child was circumcised, he was called Jesus, the name given by the angel before he was conceived in the womb."

January 1st! New Year's Day! Where in the world has another year gone? The older we get the more time flies.

Interestingly, the Church also has a special emphasis on New Year's Day. January lst is often observed as the "Name of Jesus Day."

In W.H. Auden's "Christmas Oratorio," the three Wise Men come up to the manger at the end of their long and perilous journey. When at last they stand before the Holy Family and look into the face of Jesus, Auden has them say, "O here and now our restless journey ends."

They had searched for a king. They had followed a star, and now their quest was over. To them this baby Jesus was the end of their restless quest to find the key that they believed would open a treasure chest of hope for humankind. "Oh here and now, our restless journey ends."

But that's not all. The poet completes the picture when he has the shepherds come to the manger. They also see Jesus. They say, "O here and now our restless journey starts."

I want to suggest to you that the poet is right on both accounts. The journey begins and ends in this baby named Jesus.

At the name of Jesus, "every knee should bow, and every tongue confess" that He is Lord. Here is God's expression of who God is, in a way that the world has never seen before or since. Here is the end of our searching, for those who have eyes to see. Ultimately we are called to kneel before his manger, and lay our burdens down. Here is where we see that Love, is at the heart of everything. We need to look no longer.

Yet, here, too, kneeling before the manger is where our restless journeys begin. It is the same Jesus who says, "Come to me, all you who labor and are heavy laden, and I will give you rest," who says, "Go! Deny yourselves! Take up my Cross and follow me. Love as I have loved. Forgive, as I have forgiven. Live as I have lived."

Someone has written:

> Though Christ a thousand times
> In Bethlehem be born.
> If he's not born in thee,
> Thy soul is still forlorn.

As you take the first steps of your journey this year, let them be taken in the name of Jesus, and may all your journeys in life begin and end in Him.

Prayer: Thank you, O Lord, for this Name of Jesus and what it has meant to all of us who seek to live by faith. Let him be our light today as we begin this brand New Year. And at the end of all our days, may we find our rest in Him. In the Name of Jesus we pray. Amen.

Epiphany

And we have seen his glory.

John 1:14

Hearing the Call of Jesus

Scripture: Mark 1:16-17 As Jesus passed along the Sea of Galilee, he saw Simon and his brother Andrew casting a net into the sea—for they were fishermen. And Jesus said to them, "Follow me and I will make you fish for people."

Our Gospel text tells of Jesus calling the four fishermen, Peter, Andrew, James and John.

St. Luke tells us in Acts, that Peter went on after Pentecost to become an especially significant leader in the early Christian church. He rose from the ordinary roots of his trade of fishing to become an articulate preacher and a persuasive evangelist for the faith that Jesus called him to that day.

"Follow me," said Jesus. "And I will make you fish for people." Immediately they left their nets and followed him.

These fishing texts always catch my eye. It has something to do with my love for fishing, I think, but I know I'm always impressed with these common fishermen and how their lives were turned around by that man, and those two little words, "follow me."

Not long ago, I put on my ice fishing clothes, grabbed my bucket, and headed for Lake of the Woods, our annual trek to the northland in the dead of winter. Not many people can understand that people would choose to do this, stare at a little hole in the ice for several hours, waiting for a bobber to go down, but there are quite a few of us who are crazy enough to do it. We love it!

One of the guys in our group of men that go each year is a man named Robert Duncan.

I wrote a poem about him when I got back from this particular trip, because Robert Duncan reminded us that fisher-

men and women are still being called to follow, the man, who
walked by the Sea of Galilee. Here is my poem:

Robert Duncan was his name
Fishing through the ice was his game.

A big man, Robert was,
85 years young,
With an appetite to match a man
One-fourth his age.

The restaurant was filled that night,
With burly souls of every shape and size.
Bearded, rugged men, with gnarly calloused hands,
Smoking cigarettes, drinking coffee black, and other drinks.
Hardy men, they were.
For the wilderness had called them
To their "cavemen" roots.
They were "providing" for their families back home.

There were laughing sounds, swearing sounds,
Sounds that made a preacher blush,
For you must understand these men with furry caps,
And grizzly chins,
Were only to be trusted from afar.
Then all at once, amidst the raucous din,
There came a voice, that thundered out,
And suddenly a quiet hush set in,
The likes of which amazed us all.
Robert Duncan called us all to prayer!

Hands were folded, heads were bowed,
In reverence and respect,
While Robert Duncan led us all in grace.
(It was intended for our table,
But Robert said it loud and clear.
There wasn't any doubt that all the world
Could hear!)

"Thank you Lord," he bellowed out, "For
Opportunities like these, to laugh and be together.
Thanks for each one here, and for this food
That you may strengthen us to Serve You
In everything we do. Amen."

Timidly the raucous sounds resumed,
For everyone had heard the prayer.
Our cheeks were pink, but we were proud,
That Robert Duncan set the table right.
And round the table came the glowing affirmation of
"Amen!"

Robert Duncan will forever be the chaplain of our fishing
crew. He was not afraid to let his faith be seen in this unlikely
place. He reminded all of us not to take for granted, these
graceful moments in our lives. He had heard the words that
Jesus spoke, beside the sea long ago.

**Prayer: O Spirit of the Living God, give us boldness for our
faith. Give us ears to hear your word that beckon us to
follow You, wherever we may be. Let the faith we claim, be
seen, in everything we do. We pray in Jesus Name. Amen.**

The Rock of Faith

Scripture: Matthew 16:18 "And I tell you, you are Peter, and on this rock I will build my church, and the gates of Hades shall not prevail against it."

A couple of weeks before Christmas, Emily called. You know, of course, that Emily is our granddaughter, and she was three-and-a-half at the time. I could tell she was crying, and she was crying hard. I was nervous; because I couldn't imagine what in the world was causing her to cry so hard, and why she was calling me and not her mother. Where were her mother and dad, I wondered? She was crying so hard that I couldn't understand her, but finally through the gasping sobs, I could make it out. She was crying, she said, because her Daddy forgot to hug her before he went to work. Actually, he did hug her, she sobbed, but she wanted two hugs before he went to work today. Now he was off at work and couldn't give her the hug she simply had to have.

I tried to be serious and sympathetic. But it was all that I could do to keep from chuckling. Such problems. Would that all the children in the world should have such problems as these!

After she told Grandma of her dilemma, she even wanted to call her Aunt Shelly in Alaska to tell her. That's how serious this whole thing was.

In talking to her mother later, I discovered that this was Emily's latest stalling trick before she went to bed. This wasn't the first time that she had been upset because Daddy hadn't given her at least two or three hugs before he went to work. But she was really worked up tonight! In fact, Kristina, her mother, told me that she wanted to go to the dresser in the bedroom so she could look at their wedding picture and see him and talk to him. When Kristina took her into the bedroom, Emily took the picture in her arms, held it close to her little body and said, "Oh, Daddy! When you come tomorrow I want to feel your big strong arms around me again. Daddy... my Daddy!"

I chuckled again, this time with a tear in my eye. How wonderful, even if it was a stalling technique at bedtime! How awesome that she experienced and desired that strength, that solid security of her Daddy's big strong arms around her!

That "rocklike" image of God is not a stranger to the pages of the Bible. "In you, O Lord, have I taken refuge," the Psalmist writes. "Be my strong rock, a castle to keep me safe; you are my crag and my stronghold."

It was that rocklike faith and courage that Jesus saw in Peter. It was the same strength that Emily saw in her daddy.

And when the changes of life shake us, ruffle us, and sometimes leave us with nowhere to turn, our faith reminds us that our God is like a rock. We can build our lives upon God's strength. We can place our trust in the One who is our "rock" and our salvation.

Prayer: Sometimes, O God, you seem to be so far away when life assails us, or when we lose our way in the everyday things. Put your big strong arms around us Lord, that we may feel the strength of your hug, over and over again. Assure us of that firm foundation, in the midst of transformation, that we know through your Son, Jesus Christ our Lord. Amen.

A Looking up, A Looking Down

Scripture: I Corinthians 7:31 "For the present form of this world is passing away."

Not long ago, while walking in the park, I saw a woman jogging. She wasn't running fast, but make no mistake she was running. She jogged with a certain sureness in her gait, in spite of the ice and snow that packed the path in Purgatory Park that day.

When I saw her coming, I stepped to the other side of the path to avoid a terrible collision. But when I stepped to one side, she started coming toward me once again. So I moved back once more. Then she did too. We were doing a dance on the trail of the park that day, without a dance band! My mind said that this could be trouble.

At last she saw me. I greeted her with my friendliest pastor's voice. "Oh," she said with a foolish smile, "I guess I had better look up."

I walked on, smiling. Thinking about her words. Thankful we hadn't had a fender bender out on the trail.

"It's true," I said to myself. "It's good to be looking up. But when you're jogging on an icy trail, it's also pretty important to be looking down."

I thought about an article that I had just read on optimism. Optimists are *looking up* kinds of people. I remember reading that optimists live longer than pessimists and that they are usually higher performers. I remembered reading that in the past three decades there were 46,000 professional psychological papers on depression and just 400 on joy.

The essence of the article was that in the century that lies ahead all of this was going to change. In the twenty-first century psychologists would be spending far more time *looking up* than *looking down*.

I think that people of faith have always looked on the positive side of life. We have been called to see life in a new way. We have heard the voice of God, whispering, even in the darkest of our times. Along with St. Paul, we believe, "that the present form of this life is fading away." A new world is busy being born.

But this is not to say that as Christians we don't also need to be *looking down*. We need to see the realities of life. We need to face them, and accept them as they are. The pathways of our lives can be icy and treacherous sometimes. We need to be very much aware of the conditions, lest we fall. But even as we look *down*, in faith we see the One who leads us through these treacherous conditions.

When I read the cartoons I try not to miss "Crankshaft." He's a crabby old man, with a soft and tender heart who drives a school bus. He's a grouchy old curmudgeon, that you would hardly call an optimist. Yet you know that deep inside there is a heart of mush. The children who ride his bus are afraid of him, and yet they love him. He holds the world's record for destroying mailboxes on his route.

Not long after driving his bus through a terrible storm, we saw the old curmudgeon coming in to his loving daughter's home where he lives. The last child on the bus that day was a deeply troubled one. As they begin to talk, "Crankshaft" discovers that she had no one to go home to in the midst of the storm. There was no one waiting at the end of the line who cares for her.

With the voice of that child still echoing in his mind, her pain still etched in his heart, Crankshaft enters the door of his home. He is greeted with a warm and loving hug from his daughter, a woman who loves him dearly in spite of his crotchety ways.

"This storm is supposed to be bad. I'm glad you're home safely, Dad."

"Yeah", he growls, "I'm glad to be home."

As he puts his coat in his closet that night he says: "You know, sometimes the things you take for granted are the things you would have wanted all along, if you had been smart enough to realize it in the first place."

Even old Crankshaft is given a glimpse now and then that "the present form is fading away." Somewhere deep inside he's heard the whisper of a greater call.

Prayer: Thank you, O Lord, for your gift of unspeakable joy. Life is good, but life is also hard. We need to be "looking up" and "looking down", but help us to see Your face in the midst of both, today and always. We pray in Jesus Name. Amen.

The Light Breaks In

Scripture: Isaiah 58:10 "If you offer your food to the hungry, and satisfy the needs of the afflicted, then your light shall rise in the darkness and your gloom like the noonday."

If you're anything at all like me, you've enjoyed getting up in the morning and seeing the sun come up just a little earlier each day. And in the evening, we know that our days are getting longer, and the sun stays with us, just a little more every day.

That's a hopeful sign. Those of us who live in Minnesota, and have experienced the long Minnesota winters, look desperately for these signs each year, we long for any hints of spring that nature might afford. We are longing for the light!

"You are the light of the world," Jesus tells us in St. Matthew's Gospel. "A city built on a hill cannot be hid. No one lights a lamp, and puts it under a bushel basket, but on the lamp stand, and it gives light to all in the house. In the same way, let your light shine before others, so that they may see your good works, and give glory to your Father in heaven.

"This little light of mine, I'm gonna let it shine" we used to sing in Sunday School. "I'm gonna let it shine, let it shine, let it shine!"

In the television series called "China Beach," Colleen McMurphy is a nurse who is captured and taken behind Viet Cong lines. She is forced to operate on an old man who is wounded. They take her to an old building where there is a make-shift operating room. They demand that she perform the surgery despite her protests that she is not a doctor.

While the American forces bombard the area, and the lights went out, making it impossible for her to see anything, much less perform an operation that she has never done before.

"I need more light," she pleaded.

And so the Vietnamese people started to come, bringing candles and lanterns, one by one. Soon we have this dramatic picture of a totally dark building slowly becoming a blaze of light: from the countryside they come, from the winding pathways that surround the village in every direction. With their lights in hand, they steadily flow into the building. At the center, a life-saving operation takes place; performed by a woman who is doing so, for the very first time.

Later, as Colleen McMurphy reflects on her experience, she is touched by her own lack of connectedness, her own longing for a place to belong, and for a sense of community. With a deep sense of admiration she says, "When that old man needed them, they were there for him."

Being there for one another. . . .that's what community is all about, isn't it? That's what love is all about. That happens when each of us bring our own little candles, our own little lights, and seek to bring some brightness into the darkness of each other's world. It was Jesus who came to be "the true light, that enlightens the world." Now he calls those who follow him to be his light, wherever and whenever we can.

Prayer: You are the true light, O Christ, that has come into our world. Lighten our darkness once again. Inspire us to let our lives shine into the darkness that surrounds us. In Jesus Name. Amen.

The Greatest of These

Scripture: I Corinthian 13:13 "And now faith, hope, love abide, these three. But the greatest of these is love."

Whoever Finds This I Love You

On a quiet street in the city a little old man walked
     along,
Shuffling through the autumn afternoon,
And the autumn leaves reminded him of other summers
          Come and gone.
He had a long, lonely night ahead, waiting for June.

Then among the leaves near an orphan's home a piece
     of paper
          Caught his eye,
And he stopped to pick it up with trembling hands.
As he read the childish writing the old man began to cry
Cause the words burned inside him like a brand.

"Whoever finds this, I love you, whoever finds this I
          need you
I ain't got no one to talk to
So whoever finds this, I love you."

The old man's eyes searched the orphan's home and
          Came to rest upon a child
With her nose pressed up against the windowpane.
And the old man knew he found a friend at last, so he
          Waved to her and smiled.

And they both knew they'd spend the winter laughing
        At the rain.

And they did spend the winter laughing at the rain
Talking through the fence and exchanging little gifts
        They had made for each other.
The old man would carve toys for the little girl
She would draw pictures for him of beautiful ladies
Surrounded by green trees and sunshine, and they
        Laughed a lot.

But then on the first day of June the little girl ran to the
        Fence
To show the old man a picture she drew, but he wasn't
        There.
And somehow the little girl knew he wasn't coming back
So she went to her room, took a crayon and paper and
        Wrote...

"Whoever finds this, I love you, whoever finds this, I
        need you.
I ain't even got no one to talk to.
So whoever finds this, I love you.."

In the very last verse of the 12th chapter of 1st Corinthians, after listing all of the spiritual gifts that people have been given, St. Paul writes, "And I will show you a still more excellent way." Thus begins the 13 chapter of 1st Corinthians, his famous chapter on love. It's a chapter that ends with the words that most of us know by heart. "And now faith, hope, and love abide, these three; and the greatest of these is love."

The older I get, it seems, the more I talk about love. The older I get the more I realize how important it is to me, and how important it is to our lives. Perhaps you tire of me talking about love. But when you measure the value of love against the values that the world seems to be telling us are important, there is no comparison.

A lot of us, and I include myself when I write this, can get so concerned, so stressed out, and out of sorts when things in our lives don't go the way we planned. When the budget's looking bleak, when some of our dreams come crashing down, when the car breaks down or we feel a cold or the flu coming on, or whatever may interrupt the way we thought our life should go, St. Paul calls us back to the greatest gift of all. It's a gift that never ends.

I was feeling that way the other day, out of sorts, that is. When I took off my suit jacket that morning to begin my day, I felt some papers on the inside pocket. I pulled them out to see what they might be, hoping that I might have inadvertently stuffed some dollar bills in there. But when I looked, I decided, that what I had found, was even better.

Two little pieces of paper, scribbled with color crayons. There were two little heads, with little purple eyes, that were looking out at me. These were the masterpieces of little budding artists who were six, three, and two years old. They were gifts of love from the three cutest grandchildren in the world.

"That's what really matters," I decided. "I need to remember."

When we face the very tough tests of life, it's love that we need to rely on. It's love that pulls us through. "And I will show you a still more excellent way."

Prayer: O God, assure us of your love for us today and inspire us to learn to love each other. Thank you for this precious gift, and help us to know that the world awaits our sharing. We pray this in Jesus Name. Amen.

Lent

And he was wounded for our transgressions...

Isaiah 53:5

Looking Inside of Ourselves

Psalm 51:10 "Create in me a clean heart, O God, and renew a right spirit within me."

I read about Hugh Thompson in the paper the other day. Have you ever heard of him? If you read the article, perhaps you have. Otherwise, probably not.

The odds are you have heard of Lt. William Calley. The odds are you have heard of the My Lai massacre.

It seems as though Hugh Thompson was about to receive the "Soldier's Medal," a medal that's given to those who risk their lives in situations where an opposing army is not involved. It has taken Hugh Thompson almost thirty years to get it.

It was the same war and the same place and even the same time that William Calley became a household word that Hugh Thompson earned his "Soldier's Medal." His story is the one sliver of light in the midst of that dark, dark, day.

My Lai was deceptively quiet that March day. Thompson and his crew were to swoop down over the village and draw fire so helicopters behind them could destroy the enemy with machine gun and rocket fire. They never drew fire. But they spotted a young Vietnamese girl, injured and lying on the road. Thompson marked the spot with a smoke grenade, radioed for help and then hovered nearby.

He and his crew watched in horror as an American Army officer walked up to the girl, flipped her over with his foot, and shot her dead.

They saw bodies of Vietnamese children, women and old men piled up in an irrigation ditch. Thompson landed and implored American soldiers to help the wounded. Instead, troops fired into the bodies. Thompson wracked his brain for an explanation. "We wanted to find some reason to blame the enemy," he said, "but it just didn't work. It all added up to something that we just didn't want to believe." He was moved to action when he spotted villagers crowded in a hut; an old woman was standing in the doorway, a baby in her arms. They were looking to him. He decided at once that there was no way that he could turn his back on them.

When he told the officer in charge to help him get the villagers out, the officer told him that the only help the villagers were going to get was a hand grenade. So Thompson placed his chopper down in front of the advancing Americans, and gave his gunner, Lawrence Colburn, a simple direct order. He told him to train his M-60 on the American GIs. Colburn was ordered to "open up on them" if they attempted to harm the villagers. Then Thompson radioed to two gun ships behind him, and together they airlifted a dozen villagers to safety.

Flying back to the irrigation ditch where his other crewmate, Glen Andreotta, saw something move. Andreotta jumped out and waded through the bodies, until he reached a two-year-old boy, still clinging to his mother. The standoff lasted 15 minutes. Thompson fought off tears as he told about that two-year-old boy in a complete state of shock being pulled away from his dead mother. "I had a son at home about the same age," he said through his tears.

Few Americans ever knew of Thompson's deed until David Egan, a professor emeritus at Clemson University, saw a British Broadcasting documentary on My Lai ten years ago in which Thompson was interviewed. The professor began to write hundreds of letters, pleading that the story be told, and the proper recognition given.

Why the delay? Well, the Pentagon blamed it on the bureaucracy. Others would say it's because as a nation, we can't face the shocking truth that we could possibly be guilty of such a horrible massacre, shameful deed.

Sometimes it's hard to look inside ourselves and see the truth. Lent calls us to do that; to look inside, and see the horrible truth of the things that all of us are capable of.

Hugh Thompson and Lawrence Colburn are returning to My Lai. They are to receive a reward from the people. They hope to find that little boy who was two-years-old, and say they are sorry.

Prayer: Lead us, O God, in this Lenten season, not to be afraid to look inside of ourselves as individuals, as nations, and communities who are still searching how to live with each other. Give us the courage to see the darkness and to seek your forgiveness. Lift up heroes like Hugh Thompson and his crew, who will hold a mirror before us, to help us see. "Create in me a clean heart, O God, and renew a right spirit within me." In Jesus Name. Amen.

Hope Through Suffering

Scripture: Romans 5: 3-5 "And not only that, but we also boast in our sufferings, knowing that suffering produces endurance, and endurance produces character, and character produces hope, and hope does not disappoint us, because God's love has been poured into our hearts through the Holy Spirit that has been given us."

I watched my father try to write his name last week.

It was something all of us have done and do,
    With ease, without an effort or a thought.

He, too, could do it easily, once.
Though Dad was never one for writing very much at all.

Each letter was given the utmost concentration now.
Each one, painfully searching for the line, and for the shape,
    That would spell out who He was, and had been.

As I watched his shaking, weakened hand try desperately to
    Shape the letters of his name that day,
I thought about the strength those hands once held,
    The nails they pounded as they built our home,
    The well they drilled with driving force,
    The beams they held in place, as dreams took shape.

When I was a boy it seemed as though there wasn't anything
    Dad's hands
        Couldn't do
  Or fix
  Or build.

And now I watched for ten long minutes,
    Just to see him sign his name.

"You can do it Dad," I said inside. "I know you can,
    You've always done it in the past."

The paper he was signing?
They were his entrance papers, to a strange new home.
Not the one his hands had built, but this one, this home
    Would be a place for those who couldn't do these things.
A home for those who needed help in living out the later years.

It was hard to watch my father try to sign his name last week.
    My eyes were filled with tears.

In St. Paul's letter to the Romans, he talks about "knowing
that suffering produces endurance, and endurance produces
character, and character produces hope, and hope does not
disappoint us, because God's love has been poured into our
hearts through the Holy Spirit."

Dad knows this. He believes it. He lives it. There is a hope
within him that will not disappoint him. Thank God.

**Prayer: Sustain us, O Lord, and be our sure rock, as we
experience the sufferings of our lives. Keep our eyes focused
on the Cross, knowing as we do, that you enter these painful
stages with us, fully, in the person of your Son, through
whom your living Hope has come, does come, and will come
again. Through Christ our Lord. Amen.**

Setting Our Minds on the Spirit

Scripture: Romans 8:6 "To set the mind on the flesh is death, but to set the mind on the Spirit is life and peace."

In St. Paul's letter to the Romans he writes: "To set the mind on the flesh is death, but to set the mind on the Spirit is life and peace."

"Setting our minds on the Spirit," it seems to me, is what we as baptized Christians need to always be about. We need to be about looking for the ways that the Spirit of God is moving among us, and within us. Whatever the season of our church year, we need to be watching for the signs, even if only they are tiny glimpses, each and every day of our lives.

The author Megan McKenna helps us to do that as she shares with us the following story:

"Once upon a time there was a little boy who had been going to Sunday school for years. After hearing about God for so long, he decided it was time to go look for God himself. He thought the journey might be long, so he found an old gym bag that was his father's; he stocked up on root beer, granola bars, and Snackwells; and then he set off, without telling his mother where he was going. He was about six years old. Well, he hadn't gotten very far when he got tired and decided to rest a while.

There was a park right there, and he cut across the grass to a bench. There was only one other person in the park, an old, old woman who was sitting on the bench. He climbed up beside her. The two sat there and didn't say anything for the longest time. Then he turned to her and asked her if she was thirsty. She smiled at him and nodded. Out came the root beer. They shared and sat in silence. Then they ate the cookies and granola bars and finished the root beer. They were together about an hour, and she didn't say anything at all, just smiled at him every once in a while. So he talked. He told stories of his mom and dad, brothers and sisters, his first year at school, his pets, everything.

Time passed and he thought of his mother at home. He realized that she'd be furious at him for going off without telling her, so he decided he had better go home. He got down from the bench and picked up his empty bag. They had finished everything. He said goodbye to the old woman and turned to go away. He took a few steps and stopped. He thought to himself, 'She has such a lovely smile. I want to see it again.'

So he turned around, ran up to her, put his arms around her, and gave her a big hug and kiss. Her face broke out in a magnificent smile. He smiled back and headed for home.

His mother was waiting for him at the door, frantic. She grabbed hold of him and shook him. "Where were you? I told you never to go off without telling me. Where have you been? I've been worried sick."

He looked at her and smiled broadly. "You didn't have to worry. I spent the afternoon in the park with God!" Momentarily stunned, his mother was speechless. He continued thoughtfully, "You know, I never thought she'd be so old and so quiet...and thirsty."

Meanwhile, the old woman had gotten up very slowly from her bench, picked up her cane, and headed for home. Her son, about forty-five years old, was waiting for her.

"Mother," he said, "how many times do I have to tell you not to go off on your own without telling me? I've been looking for you everywhere and was just about to call the paramedics and the police again. You can't just go wandering off. Where have you been?"

Her face was radiant. She smiled at him and said, "Oh, you needn't have worried. I spent the afternoon in the park with God."

Her son was stunned and thought to himself. "Oh, dear. She's much worse than before."

But she continued, rather thoughtfully. "You know, I didn't expect him to be so young and so talkative. . . . and to love root beer!"

Prayer: Where are you, O God? Where are the signs of your living among us? So often it seems we look for you in all the wrong places. Help us to open ourselves, like a little child, to see you in the eyes and in the hearts of those with whom our lives entwine. Give us the vision of the elders in our midst, who have learned through seasoned time that you are always on the prowl, looking for us, and waiting to be seen. Set our minds and our eyes on the Spirit, that we may know life and peace. In Jesus Name. Amen.

I Love to Tell the Story

Scripture: John 3:16 "For God so loved the world, that he gave his only begotten Son, that whoever believes in Him should not perish but have everlasting life."

From William White's book, *Stories for the Journey* there comes an anonymous little story that is simply called, "The Chosen People."

> The Lord decided to select a nation to be his chosen people. And first he interviewed the Greeks. "If I was to be your God and you were to be my people, what could you do for me?" the Lord God asked.
>
> "O Lord," the Greek people replied, "If you were to be our God and we were to be your people, we would honor you with the finest art and loftiest systems of thought. Our great thinkers would extol you in their great writings."
>
> "Thank you for your offer," the Lord said.
>
> Next God visited the Romans. "If I were to be your God and you were to be my people, what could you do for me?" he asked.
>
> "Great King of the Universe," the Romans said, "we are a nation of builders. If you were to be our God and we were to be your people, we would erect great buildings in your name and wonderful road systems so that your people could travel to worship in these great buildings."
>
> The Lord seemed pleased with the offer and thanked the Romans.
>
> From Rome the Lord went all over the world, interviewing one nation after another. Finally he interviewed a small Mideastern group, the Jews, who had a reputation for being shrewd traders.

Once again the Lord asked his question. "If I was to be your God and you were to be my people, what could you do for me?"

"Lord," the Jewish people said. "We are not known for our power or our art or our buildings. However, we are a nation of storytellers. If you were to be our God and we were to be your children, we would tell your story throughout the whole world."

God, who also had a reputation for being a shrewd trader, said, "It's a deal."

I have a friend who reminds his listening audience every time he tells them a story, that "all of his stories are true, and some of them actually happened."

He's right. Stories are a marvelous way of communicating the truth. And certainly the stories of our faith have communicated to all of us God's truth, God's wisdom, God's will, as God would have us know it.

During the Lenten season we have developed this marvelous tradition of hearing over and over again the story of our Lord's life and death. It's a story that reminds us of God's inexhaustible forgiveness for our sins, your sins and mine.

In this Holy Season, we are invited to kneel before the Cross, day after day, to confess our inhumanity to other human beings, our selfishness, and the meager kind of love with which we love each other and our God. Then we focus on a man named Jesus and a road that leads to Golgotha, a place that was called 'the skull'. Each year our story leads us to a place of death that leads to life. It's a place where we can be forgiven, and begin again.

"For God so loved the world," John writes in his Gospel, "that he gave his only begotten Son, that whoever believes in him shall not perish but have everlasting life."

It's a marvelous story. It's one that we need to hear again and again. It's one that we need to share. And it's a powerful truth.

Prayer: Thank you, Lord, for the "old, old, story, of Jesus and his love." Help us to know it as our story, and not be afraid to tell it over and over again. We pray in Jesus name. Amen.

The Road to the Cross

Scripture: Matthew 20:27 "And whoever wishes to be first among you must be your slave."

I want to share with you this great birthday card I got in the mail from my sister. On the front it said: "Happy Birthday, brother! Guess who thinks that you're the greatest guy ever? Who thinks you're the greatest gift to the world? Who thinks you could be the future President of the United States?"

And when you open up the card to the inside it says in bold letters: "Mom!" And then it says, "P.S. I kind of like you myself."

There is something about mothers and their sons, isn't there? In today's Gospel Lesson it's the mother of James and John who comes up to Jesus and says: "Grant that one of these two sons of mine may sit at your right and the other at your left in your kingdom."

Would my mother be so bold as to ask the same, I wondered? I'm not sure. But you'll have to admit her request is a bit presumptuous!

The thing is, Jesus said it isn't going to work that way. As a matter of fact, he suggested that James and John would be by his side all right, but it wouldn't be in the same way that either they or their mother had in mind.

Tradition says that the disciple James was the first of the apostolic band to die as a martyr.

"Can you drink the cup of which I have to drink?" Jesus asks them both.

For James the cup was martyrdom.

John, tradition tells us, was to live a long and disciplined Christian life. He lived to be almost a hundred years old.

Both disciples were destined to be by their Master's side, but they would walk beside him in suffering and service, not in grandeur and glory. "And whoever wishes to be first among you must be your slave."

In one of the old Zen talks, Soyen Shaku, one of the Zen Masters, walked past a house where he heard there was much crying because the master of the house lay dead. Being well known in the locality, he entered, sat down and cried with them.

Said one of those present, "Master, how can you cry? Surely you are beyond such things."

Soyen Shaku answered gently, "It is this that puts me beyond such things."

Prayer: Help us, Lord, to be your servants. Help us to see that real greatness comes when we can put ourselves aside, to wash another's feet, to listen to another's pain, to cry with them, to walk in their shoes, even though we might rather be almost any other place. Thank you for entering our lives and becoming our servant, in the person of your Son, Jesus Christ, our Lord. Amen.

Thank You

Scripture: Romans 6: 3-4 "Do you not know that all of us who have been baptized into Christ Jesus were baptized into his death? Therefore we have been buried with him by baptism into death, so that, just as Christ was raised from the dead by the glory of the Father, we too might walk in newness of life."

As I was walking up the walkway toward the central building of our Mount Olivet Retreat Center one day, I looked over to the right of the door and saw the Cross. It's a large Cross, and when the sun comes up, or the floodlights hit it just right, it casts its long shadow over the sidewalk that approaches the building. This Cross stands there, announcing who we are and why we're here.

There is a sign on the Cross. I've seen it before, but for whatever reason, I saw it that day as if I were seeing it for the very first time.

"Thank you Lord," that's all it said. Three words on that big tall Cross, and they said it all.

So many things in life are that way. You're walking along in a familiar place, and everything is just the way it's always been; then suddenly it isn't anymore. You're seeing it in a way that you've never seen it before.

The sign was simple. So were the words. "Thank you Lord."

At lunchtime that day we had been talking about some of the new trends in worship. My friend calls them the "happy clappy" types of worship. He said that one of the things that makes him sad about those kinds of worship is that there is seldom ever anything mentioned about the Cross. There is often only the glory of the Lord. There is very little about the pain or about the cost, for Jesus, and for us.

"If anyone would come after me, let them deny themselves, and take up their cross," said Jesus, "and follow me. For whoever would save their life will lose it, and whoever loses their life for my sake and the Gospel's will save it."

When I saw that sign that day, I had been thinking about my father who had died just the week before. At my Dad's funeral I heard again those words that I myself have read many times. "When we were baptized in Christ Jesus, we were baptized into his death."

We were buried with him by Baptism into death, so that as Christ was raised from the dead by the glory of the Father, we too might live a new life. For if we have been united with Him in a death like his, we shall certainly be united with him in a resurrection like his."

They were simple words that I saw on the sign that day. But so important. For my father, for me, and for all of humankind.

"Thank you Lord. Thank you for the Cross."

Prayer: For your wondrous love, O Lord, we give you thanks today. For the powerful promise that comes through the Cross, we are grateful. Help us, O Christ, to take up our Cross and follow you. We pray in Jesus Name. Amen.

Easter

He is not here...for he has been raised...

Matthew 28:6

Standing at the Edge of the Grave

Matt. 28: 8: "So they left the tomb quickly with fear and great joy, and ran to tell his disciples."

St. Matthew's Gospel describes the first day of Easter in the following way. "And suddenly there was a great earthquake; for an angel of the Lord, descending from heaven, came and rolled back the stone and sat on it. His appearance was like lightnings, and his clothing white as snow. For fear of him, the guards shook and became like dead men.

And when Mary Magdalene and the other Mary heard him speak, he said to them, "Do not be afraid; I know that you are looking for Jesus who was crucified. He is not here; for he has been raised." So they left the tomb quickly with fear and with great joy, and ran to tell his disciples."

This is a powerful message that we proclaim today!

It is far more powerful than most of us can even bear to imagine, and it has nothing at all to do with jellybeans and floppy eared and furried bunnies. It is a message of "fear" and a message of "joy."

The major celebration of Easter among the Moravians of Waconia, Minnesota, a place that I once served as pastor, used to take place in the cemetery. They called it "God's Acre."

There the saints have been buried for generations under simple white stones, bearing testimony to the simplicity of their faith and the "democracy" of death.

Between the love feasts of Holy Week and Easter morning, the people come there, to the cemetery, with brushes and pails to scrub the stones. On Holy Saturday, every stone gets a bouquet of fresh flowers.

On Easter day, before dawn, the whole community meets at the little white frame country church near the cemetery, and then to the subdued sounds of brass bands, they march to the cemetery. There, among the orderly rows of marble, in the very teeth of death, they celebrate the resurrection of Jesus Christ. It is as if that were the only proper place to have such a celebration, out there, among the tombs, where death itself is unavoidable, even in the dawning light of an April day.

I'm told it's the mood that strikes you. There is no sermon preached out there, just the familiar words of the Easter Scriptures. The celebration is understated, and there is about it a quiet waiting—for the sun to come up, and for more.

Our prevailing mood of Easter is joy. When I suggest that another context might be appropriate for our consideration; I don't want to take anything away from this day. I don't want **you** to miss the joy today, but neither do I want you to pass over lightly all of the depth and the power of what has been done here in Christ.

The message of Easter is addressed particularly to those who have stood or are standing at the edge of the grave. The deep, deep promises and the holy mystery of this morning, are given to you today.

The message of Easter is a powerful promise! It is something that we can tie our life to—and our death.

To all who stand at the edge of the grave (and that my friends is all of us!) there come these words, "He is risen! He is risen indeed!"

Prayer: We quietly wait, O Christ, in the midst of our living and dying, for the morning sun, and for more. We wait, O Christ, at the edge of our own graves, for the powerful promise of Easter. Help us again to capture the depth and the joy. We pray in Jesus name. Amen.

Facing Death's Reality

Scripture: Mark 16:6 "But he said to them, 'Do not be alarmed; you are looking for Jesus of Nazareth who was crucified. He has been raised; he is not here. Look, this is the place where they laid him."

Several years ago an intriguing little story appeared in the *New Yorker* magazine. It was the story of a man on his way home from the office on a rainy Friday evening to face a cluster of minor problems involving the various members of his family.

Among them, a teenage son who'd taken the car without permission and banged it up; a wife who had suddenly panicked by imaginary symptoms occasioned by an article on pernicious anemia she had read at her hairdresser's a day or so before; and a father who was getting too old to live as he wanted to live, alone in his own large house.

The problems were minor and familiar. He had handled them all before in the same easy way, from the expected lecture to his son, to the jocular reassurance to his wife, to the customary talk with his father about the advantages of a small, bright apartment. But on that rainy Friday evening, as he made his way home through mid-Manhattan, he happened to see a man who had just been run down by a car, lying dead in the middle of the street. And for only the second or third time in his life, the final horizon which, of course, had always lurked in the background, shadowy, and almost unreal, came sharply into focus. The conscious realization that he, too, was going to die one day, hit him like a sledgehammer. It made a difference when he got home that night.

The lecture to his son came out as expected but it seemed unreal and inconsequential as if he were not really talking to his son. Nor could he summon up the expected bantering tone with his wife to reassure her that she was plagued with imaginary demons. He tried, but it didn't come off. When he got around to his father, he gave up, and simply told him that if he wanted to live in his own big house, there was no good reason why he shouldn't. The story goes on to indicate the subtle changes that went on in the lives of this family when suddenly death became a reality in one man's life.

Most of us will do anything not to have to face that reality. We would rather not look. Death is frightening. When I meet with a family to plan a funeral, "Keep it light, pastor," they tell me. "We don't want a morose service, that's for sure."

It is reported that William Randolph Hearst who accumulated vast power and wealth during his lifetime in his publishing business, would never allow anyone to use the word death in his presence. That same taboo is present in much of life today. We frankly and openly talk about everything else except this "final horizon." As a result there is, for many of us, an underlying anxiety which infects our lives, which hardly ever even rises to the surface to be recognized for what it is, until, perhaps, you happen to run across a man lying dead on the street on a rainy Friday evening.

Writes Edmund Steimle:

There is a healthy realism about the Bible.

It doesn't hide from any of the facts of life. It looks every single one of them squarely in the eye, takes them all into account—sin, death, suffering, and then announces triumphantly, "the Lord God omnipotent reigneth."

The Easter message was at the heart of every one of those earliest sermons of the early Christian church. They were not there to proclaim simple moralisms or little bits of wisdom about how to live a good life. Those early church preachers knew that none of this mattered, until death had been brought out into the open and dealt with.

Death is a reality. Make no mistake. Our Christian faith knows that, and believes that. Yet we also know and believe, that even as we stare into the face of death in all its ugliness and tragedy and even as we see death through the tears of our own loss," we are more than conquerors through him who loved us." (Romans 8:37)

This is the Easter season! The Hope is ours. "He is not here. Look, there is the place where they laid him!" Praise God!

Prayer: We go along, O God, from day to day, trying not to see. Yet we know it's true. Death waits for us. It waits for me. Help us to see O God, that we may never learn to live, until we also learn that we are dying. Thank you for the victory that takes us into the face of death and beyond. Through Christ our Lord. Amen.

Faith that is Found in Honest Doubt

Scripture: John 20:27-28 "Then he said to Thomas, 'Put your finger here and see my hands. Reach out your hand and put it in my side. Do not doubt, but believe' Thomas answered him, "My Lord, and my God!"

It was the English poet Alfred Lord Tennyson who wrote: "There lives more faith in honest doubt, believe me, than in all the creeds."

The first Sunday after Easter has traditionally been the Sunday when we hear the story of Thomas. Thomas, the disciple of Jesus, who has come to be known as "the doubter."

You know the story. Until he saw him, until he saw the place where the nails had been driven into his hands and the place that the sword had entered his side, Thomas would not believe.

But the story of "doubting" Thomas is not complete until we hear his words, "My Lord, and my God!"

William Barclay relates a legend about Thomas.

After the death of Jesus, the disciples divide the country to preach the Gospel. India, that mysterious land far away, fell to Thomas. At first Thomas refused to go. He said, "I am not strong enough for the long journey."

"I am a Hebrew man," he continued, sounding a lot like Moses when God's call came to him. "How can I go amongst the Indians and preach the truth?"

Jesus appeared to Thomas by night and said, "Fear not, Thomas, go Thou unto India and preach the word there. For my grace is with Thee." But still Thomas, true to his character, refused to go.

Now it so happened that there had come to the land a certain merchant from India, sent by King Gundophorus, king of India at the time. He had come seeking a skilled carpenter and his assignment was to bring him back to India, and Thomas was a carpenter. Jesus appeared to this merchant now as well, and he told him that he had a slave who was a carpenter. The merchant signed a slip of paper that sold Thomas to the King. When he asks Thomas if Jesus is his Master, Thomas replied, "Indeed, he is!" When he ultimately discovers that he has been sold by Jesus, he finally, reluctantly, agrees to go.

The story goes on to tell how the King of India commands Thomas to build him a palace, and Thomas responds by telling him that he was able to do so. The king gave him plenty of money to buy materials and hire the workmen, but Thomas gave it all away to the poor. Always he told the king that the palace was rising steadily. Needless to say, the king was suspicious. When his messengers told him that they saw no signs of a palace anywhere in the kingdom, he sent for Thomas once more. "Have you built me a palace?" he demanded. Thomas answered, "Yes." "When shall we go and see it?" the king asked. Thomas answered, "You cannot see it now, but when you leave this life, then you will see it."

At first the king is very angry, and Thomas was in danger of his life. But in the end the king, too, was won for Christ, and so Thomas is said to have brought Christianity to India.

Now I said the story was a legend. This much, however, is certain. The Thomist church in South India still traces its origin to this reluctant disciple.

Faith was never an easy thing for Thomas. He had to be sure. He had to count the cost. Once he had, Thomas was the man who went to ultimate limit of faith and obedience.

"There lives more faith in honest doubt," said Tennyson, "believe me, than in all the creeds." The questions of life are real. There is so much that many of us will never understand, and that will always remain a mystery."[1]

The story of Thomas reminds all of us not to be afraid of our questions. We are invited instead to ask them, live them, and see them through. All the while keeping our eyes on that which we believe, however haltingly, to be closer to the Truth than anything we have ever known before, and follow Him, not even knowing where he might lead.

Prayer: The questions of faith and life surround us, Lord. Sometimes we just can't see nor can we know the answers. Our faith is weak, and sometimes trembles deep inside. We do believe, O Christ. But please, oh please, be with us in our unbelief! We pray in Christ's name. Amen.

---

1 Barclay, William. Gospel of John (2). Westminster, John Knox 1955.

A Resurrection Kind of Moment

Scripture: John 21:19 "After this he said to him, 'Follow me.'"

After Jesus was raised from the dead, John's Gospel shares with us several of his resurrection appearances. On one occasion, right after he had had breakfast with his disciples, Jesus speaks to Peter alone. In that conversation he asks Peter three times if he loves him, no doubt painfully reminding Peter of the three times he had denied him on the night before he died.

The third time he is asked, Peter is getting pretty exasperated with Jesus' questioning, but still the question comes another time. "Do you love me?" Each time Peter is asked, he assures him of his love, and Jesus responds, "Feed my sheep." After that third question he also adds these two simple words, "follow me."

The Gospel writers all tell us that there is something about "following" Jesus that leads us to experience his living presence. But that's not always easy to do.

Not long ago I saw a movie that was based on a true story. I had read about the central character in the paper. It was a touching story then, and was a touching story in the movie as well.

His name was Alvin Straight. He lived on a neat but humble farm in West Central Iowa, near the town of Laurens. The title of the film was *The Straight Story*.

Alvin hears about his brother who has had a stroke. His brother lives in Mount Zion, Wisconsin, just west of Prairie Du Chien, hundreds of miles away. He decides he has to go. The problem is that he can't see very well anymore, and so he's lost his driver's license, and he has very little money.

However, he scrapes together what he can, and buys an old John Deere riding mower, and he hooks a makeshift trailer behind it. He packs a cooler with some wieners and a few cigars; adding his two canes, because he can barely walk, he starts off to see his brother.

Sound crazy? Well it was. But he went anyway. Along back roads he drove that John Deere riding mower with the trailer on the back, sleeping at night in whatever empty field he could find at the end of the day. In the morning, he started the mower and stoked a fresh cigar and was off again.

The best part of the story though for me is the reason that Alvin feels he has to go. He had had a falling out with his brother, Lyle, about 10 years earlier. Too much drink, too much anger, and too many things had been spoken that hurt too deeply. They hadn't talked since then. Alvin didn't want either of their lives to end that way.

Rattling around in his mind were the memories of the two of them growing up together. They worked hard on their parents' farm helping them to eke out a living in poverty conditions. At night they would lay awake and watch the stars and talk, sharing a friendship that was deep through all those growing-up days. That bond was too important, Alvin had decided, not to try to save it.

It was a pretty understated movie actually. When he finally got to his brother's farm, after weeks on the road, he stood out in the yard and called his name. "Lyle?" He called. For a long time we heard nothing in the house.

Finally, a voice from inside. "Alvin?" After a long waiting pause, his brother came out. Dragging his stroke stricken body through the door, and onto the front porch, they looked at each other, and at first said nothing at all.

There was no handshake. There were no words. The audience is left waiting and wondering whether they will come to blows, will they hug, or just what will they do?

"Sit down," his brother, Lyle, ordered, and Alvin pulled an old rickety chair over from the back of the porch.

Then Lyle looked out into the yard and saw that John Deere mower sitting there with the ramshackle trailer on the back.

There was a long, long, silence. You can see him trying to process the meaning of all of this. Finally when you can stand the silence no longer, the barest of words, "You came all the way to see me on that?"

Alvin nodded. No smiles. The camera zooms back on the scraggled beard and wrinkled face of Lyle, who simply looks out at the mower one more time. He shakes his head in disbelief. The movie ended.

No golden sunsets. No last scenes with the two of them arm-in-arm. No hugs or tears. That was not to be the way of reconciling for these two crusty old brothers. One of the two had swallowed his pride. That was enough. It would have been phony if it had ended any other way. There was just the peace you felt. The forgiveness you saw in both of their eyes. It was a quiet and wondrous kind of moment. A resurrection kind of moment, not unlike that between Peter and Jesus. And the movie ended.

Prayer: In our weakness, O God, we have failed to be your messengers of forgiveness and hope in the world. Brighten the darkened corners of the lives we live with moments of resurrection that we find in following You. In Jesus Name. Amen.

Living and Dying for Others

Scripture: John 15:12-13 "This is my commandment, that you love one another as I have loved you. No one has greater love than this, to lay down one's life for his friends."

At a recent retreat for "Writers and Readers" at the Mount Olivet Retreat Center, the author David Haynes asked those of us who were there a question: "Who or what would you be willing to give your life for?" That would be a good question with which to begin, he suggested, before we begin to write about anything.

I was troubled by his question. Troubled, I think, because a ready answer didn't pop into my mind. I thought about my family. I thought about my wife, my children, my grandchildren, my mother and my sisters. I think I would be willing to give my life for them. I believe I would. But then, I like so many who have lived safely and freely in our western world, have never been put to the test. As for other causes, my country, my values, my faith, a stranger whom I have never seen, I was far less certain.

It was Elie Weisel who once said, "Our society will be judged on how we relate to strangers." Our most recent track record hasn't been that great.

"Who or what would you be willing to give your life for?" In the insulated world in which I live, I have never had to answer that question face to face. Said Jesus, "No one has greater love than this, to lay down one's life for his friends." What's even more remarkable is that, for Jesus, a world of strangers had become his friends.

Jim Wallis, in his book, *Who Speaks for God?* tells a story that he had heard on the radio.

A reporter was covering the conflict in the middle of Sarajevo, Yugoslavia, and he saw a little girl shot by a sniper. The reporter threw down his pad and pencil and stopped being a reporter for a few minutes. He rushed to the man who was holding the child and helped them both into his car.

As the reporter stepped on the accelerator, racing to the hospital, the man holding the bleeding child said, "Hurry my friend, my child is still alive!"

A moment or two later, "Hurry my friend, my child is still breathing!"

A moment later, "Hurry my friend, my child is still warm!"

Finally, "Hurry. Oh, God, my child is getting cold!"

When they got to the hospital, the little girl was dead. As the two men were in the lavatory, washing the blood off their hands and their clothes, the man turned to the reporter and said, "This is a terrible task for me. I must go tell her father that his child is dead. He will be heartbroken."

The reporter was amazed. He looked at the grieving man and said, "I thought she was your child.'

The man looked back and said, "No. But aren't they all our children?"

Yes, they are all our children. They are also God's children. He has entrusted us with their care in Sarajevo, in Somalia, in New York City, in Los Angeles, in Washington, D.C., and in Minneapolis"

Prayer: O God, help us to see the children of our world as our own children. Let us not be dulled or numbed by the sadness and the sorrow of our world, but allow us instead to feel their pain and increase our love as you have called us to do. The world is watching us, O Lord, and so are you. You call us to let the living Christ of Easter shine in each of us. In Jesus name. Amen.

You Didn't Use All Your Strength

Scripture: John 15:4-5 "Abide in me as I abide in you. Just as the branch cannot bear fruit by itself unless it abides in the vine, neither can you, unless you abide in me."

The word "abide" is an important one in John's Gospel. It appears again and again in his story of the life of Jesus. In the letters of John it's the same. "Abiding in Him" seems to be one of his central concerns. In other translations the words "dwell", or "stay" or "remain" have been chosen. But the Greek root is the same, 'meno', "to abide".

When I read this text again and listened to it speak to me, I couldn't help but think of that beautiful and timeless hymn, that's often sung at the close of the day:

> Abide with me, fast falls the eventide,
> The darkness deepens, Lord with me abide.
> When other helpers fail and comforts flee,
> Help of the Helpless, O abide with me."

A grandmother tells us about her two granddaughters. They were four and five when they had to sleep the first night in their new room. They were afraid to be in the room alone. After their mother had tucked them in their double bed, and assured them several times that all was safe, she finally said, "Remember, you're never alone. God is always with you." As she left she overheard the four-year-old say, "Move over, Courtney. Let God sleep in the middle!"

"Abiding in Him" is something like that. It's something like moving over and letting God sleep in the middle. It's the simple insight of a four-year-old that's more profound than any preacher.

To abide in Jesus is to be fully present to the presence of God in our lives and in our world. Abiding is about praying, to be sure. It's prayer not in the sense of our going to God with our grocery list of needs and concerns. But rather it's prayer, in the sense of allowing ourselves to breathe in the Spirit of Christ, allowing His Spirit to fill us with a breath that is even more life-giving than our own.

Sometime ago, Joan and I were invited to stay overnight at the home of some friends on the beautiful shores of Lake Superior in northern Minnesota. In one of the bedrooms of their home, I happened to notice a plaque that hung on their wall. It hung beside a window overlooking that majestic lake that has come to be so loved by so many. It was a framed inscription that was simply called, "To Pray."

> To pray is to
> Laugh
> Whistle
> Dance on happy feet
> Sing
> Shout
> And jump higher than
> Ever before.
> But it is also to
> Whisper
> Stumble in dark places
> Cry
> Scream
> Or just hold a worried head
> In tired hands and wait.
>
> Prayer is our tired reaching out to the One
> Who holds us closer and loves us more than
> We would ever dare to imagine. (Anonymous)

When we pray like this, we "abide in Him."
The following story says it still another way.

A boy and his father were walking along a road when they came across a large stone. The boy said to his father, "Do you think if I use all my strength I can move this rock?"

His father answered, "If you use all your strength, I am sure that you can do it." The boy began to push the rock. Exerting himself as much as he could, he pushed and pushed. The rock did not move. Discouraged, he said to his father, "You were wrong. I can't do it." His father placed his arm around the boy's shoulder and said, "No son. You didn't use all your strength...you didn't ask me to help." (David Wolpe-"Teaching Your Children about God" from *Spiritual Literacy*)

Prayer: Abide with us, O Savior. Allow us to enter the fullness of your presence, and to be lifted by a strength that is greater than our own. Help us to "move over" and let you sleep in the middle. We pray in Jesus name. Amen.

Looking at the Trees

Scripture: Psalm 8: "When I look at your heavens, the work of your fingers, the moon and the stars that you have established; what are human beings that you are mindful of them, mortals that you care for them?"

We were driving home from our cabin the other day when my wife Joan said, "Look at the trees!"

I did look. And suddenly I realized that within a day or two (or was it an hour?) at the most, all had changed. These trees had suddenly burst into life! Two days earlier, there was only the barest hint of green. Now that which was dead was born again.

If Joan hadn't said, "Look at the trees!" I wonder when or if I would have noticed at all.

Suddenly, I was very much aware. Now it almost seemed as though the green was growing, buds were popping, right before my eyes. Everywhere I looked, the sleeping winter seemed to be waking, yawning, stretching its arms, to greet the warm.

"Look at the tress!" she said.

Sometimes we need someone else to help us see.

There are so many things, it seems, that keep us from noticing, so many "tugs" upon our lives. There are the tugs of health concerns, either for ourselves or those we love. There are the tugs of our care giving to elderly parents, their quality of living. There are the tugs of parenting, a task that for most of us continues for as long as either our children or we are still alive. There are the tugs of our personal vocations, our lives in the work force. There are the day-in and day-out kinds of things, causing anxiety, creating pressures and uncertainties about our future. Not the least of those "tugs" which affect us are those that urge us to get ahead, to be better or the best, to outdo our neighbors or our friends, to have the most, or at the very least to have all those things that the world tells us that we need in order to be happy.

In a monthly publication of a newsletter (*Marsh Monthly*) for which she writes, Ruth Stricker shares with us a metaphor in the form of a story that was originally shared by Stevie Ray.

In the movie *Robinson Crusoe*, Crusoe grew tired of just sitting around and enjoying the island fruits, swimming in the ocean tide, and laying on the sunny beach. He captured a man called "Friday" from a local tribe in order to "educate" him. He taught him the English language (of course, he wouldn't learn Friday's) and strove to teach him how to be civilized. Friday had already helped build everything they needed for shelter, food, and water.

Not being civilized like the England-born Crusoe, he didn't know that life was still incomplete. Civilized nations know that life is not meant to be enjoyed, it is meant to be conquered.

Crusoe decided that they would have their own mini Olympics. First he set up a race. He said, "We will both run to that tree. The better runner wins."

"Wins what?" asked Friday.

"The race of course." Replied Crusoe.

"Why do we race?"

"Because we want to know who the better runner is."

"Why?"

"It is important to know who is best at things."

"Isn't it enough to know that we are both good?"

"No! Now stop asking stupid questions and let's begin. We are going to see who the better runner is. Ready. Set. Go!"

The two men started running. Crusoe with his arms and legs pumping madly, gulping for air as his face grimaced tightly. Friday ran almost as if he was dancing, his legs flying and arms swinging in the wind. A huge smile on his face. Crusoe got to the tree far ahead of Friday and hunched over gasping for breath as he waited for his opponent to arrive.

When Friday finally made it to the tree he said, "I win!"

"Are you mad?" Crusoe cried. "I was here long before you. How can you think you won?"

"You said the better runner would win the race. I saw how you ran. You ran as if a wild boar were chasing you. You strained every muscle and you did not enjoy one bit of your running. Now you stand there hardly able to breathe and in pain. I let my body be happy while running. I let my legs run beautifully like they were made to do, not jamming them into the ground like you. I breathed the air deep so my face could smile. You looked like you were going to faint any moment. Clearly I am the better runner because I enjoyed it."

"But I got to the tree first!" cried Crusoe. "I am the faster runner. I win."

"Ah, you did not say the 'faster' runner would win, you said the 'better'. Besides, what good is getting to the tree first if you can't enjoy yourself when you get there?"

As we watch the dawning of another spring, are we so busy trying to get to the tree first so that we're losing the race? In the movie, Ray comments, *"Friday lived to be a happy, healthy old man. Crusoe commits suicide."*

Let's pay attention to these things. Perhaps we can begin by looking at the trees.

Let us pray: Deepen our spiritual lives, O Lord. We are thirsty for the nectar of your presence! The buds are popping, the flowers bloom, and the grass is growing. Dare us not to miss these things, and stir us to be pointers of your wondrous presence! We pray in Jesus name.

What Happens When He is Gone

Scripture: Luke 24:51 "While he was blessing them, he withdrew from them, and was carried up into heaven."

Some churches still call the "Seventh Sunday of Easter" the "Sunday after the Ascension." Last Thursday was the designated "Day of the Ascension." Though few churches still observe that day with worship, we still confess, "He ascended into heaven," in the Apostle's Creed.

It's that event that St. Luke describes, both in the 24th chapter of his Gospel, and in the first chapter of the book of Acts. (1:9) After forty days on this earth, the author tells us, "he was lifted up, and a cloud took him out of sight."

You can almost hear the disciples murmuring among themselves. "What does this mean? What do we do now? Here we thought he was alive, and with us forever, and now he's gone again! What's a disciple to do?"

Jesus told them to wait; wait until they received power from on high. And wait they did, until the amazing day of Pentecost, which followed ten days later.

Listen to our prayer for today: "Almighty and eternal God, your Son our Savior is with You in eternal glory. Give us faith to see that, true to his promise, he is among us still, and will be with us to the end of time; who lives and reigns with you and the Holy Spirit, one God, now and forever. Amen.

"Give us faith to see, that true to his promise, he is among us still...."

Each year in May I like to participate in the "Walk For Kids." Joan and I walked together last year, and even though we were walking for kids, we were also walking for ourselves—for our own health, as well as our own well being.

It was a lush and lovely morning in May. It was exciting to be gathered at the starting point with walkers and runners alike. Our own daughter Amy and her good friend Jackie would be among those who were running, and there were prizes being offered for those who did well in their division.

Our senior pastor Paul Youngdahl, with his long and lanky legs, led the lusty group of walkers onward. The two of us, my wife and I, soon found ourselves falling into a comfortable pace. It was a brisk pace for two who were getting close to being called "Senior Citizens," but we were thankful to be there and to be able to walk at all.

It wasn't long before we noticed that our pace seemed to be about the same as another couple who was walking that morning. He was blind. In his left hand he carried a leash to a Golden Retriever—his companion and eyes. His other hand was linked through the arm of a woman. We discovered that she was his dear friend and other companion. We learned that the dogs name was "Hoppy." He was Bruce. She was JoAnn. It wasn't long before a lively conversation bubbled up among the four of us.

What was amazing about that walk is that Bruce, who was blind, walked just as fast as we did, from beginning to end, and stride for stride. He walked without fear, trusting "Hoppy," and trusting his friend. As he walked, he shared with us his life, and we shared ours with him, never missing a beat.

This was a man who could have easily become embittered by the cards that he'd been dealt. It was clear that wasn't the case at all. He was a gourmet cook, a gifted pianist, and a cross-country skier. He sang in his church choir. He was so attuned to the smells and the voices around him. He was more aware of that morning in May, I daresay, than any other walker that day.

He walked with purpose. He walked with hope. He walked without fear. He walked as one who knew that Christ was there, and would be "to the end of time." As we walked with him, all of us had a profound sense that the Spirit of Christ was "among us still."

I have another image from that day. There was a young woman who was also walking around the lake, but who was going the opposite way. She wasn't a part of our "Walk for Kids," but there seemed to be a definite bounce to her walk, as if she was planning to win. She was smiling radiantly, and seemed especially alive to me. Suddenly, she blurted out, to no one in particular, but to anyone who would listen, "I'm getting married today!" and then she floated by, as if in a dream.

"I'm getting married today!" she said. She said it with all of the hopes and the dreams and the purpose that come with being in love. She said it with such sheer and utter delight that we were lifted away on the wings of romance.

It was a walk for kids. We were there together: Bruce, who was blind, his very good friend, Joann, "Hoppy," his dog, Joan and I, and a charming young woman with the happiest heart I've ever seen.

It was one of those times that are all too rare, it seems. One of those times when you are fully aware, that no matter where Christ may have once disappeared to, he was true to his promise, and is among us still. So we walked on and we were not afraid.

Prayer: Thank you for those times in our lives, O Christ, when you come to, as on the wings of butterflies. Thank you for those times in our lives when the reality of presence comes wrapped in a morning, in a walk, in a smile, and a day in Spring. Help us to see and to know that you are among us still, and will be, to the end of time. Amen.

Pentecost

**So if you have been raised with Christ
seek the things that are above...**

Colossians 3:1

The Word is Very Near

Scripture: Deuteronomy 30:14 "No, the Word is very near to you; it is in your mouth and in your heart for you to observe."

Where and how does God speak to us today? Sometimes it seems as though God hardly speaks at all. It's as though the forces of sin and evil overpower the Word. Or are they overpowering our hearing of it?

"Though the wicked grow like weeds," the Psalmist says, "and all the workers of iniquity flourish, they flourish only to be destroyed forever, but you, O Lord, are exalted forever." (Psalm 92:6-7 LBW)

And so sometimes it seems to us, that the "wicked grow like weeds" and the "workers of iniquity are flourishing" while the Word of God is barely heard among us.

I thought about that again as I read the morning paper one day. Then I thought about it more as I heard a gasp from across my breakfast table. With a catch in her voice, Joan began to read the story of a father who had doused his two-year-old daughter with gasoline and set her on fire. Was it just a week before that we read the story of a mother who drowned her five beautiful children, in the midst of her battle with mental illness? And every day it seems the same. It does, in fact, seem as though the power of evil is getting the upper hand, and the voice of God is deathly silent.

Where and how does God speak in such a world of weeds? The writer of the Book of Deuteronomy in our Scripture asks essentially the same question. "Who will go up to heaven for us, and get it for us, (this Word of God) that we may hear it and observe it?

"Neither is it (this Word of God) beyond the sea, that you should say, 'Who will cross to the other side of the sea for us, so that we may hear it and observe it?' No, the Word is very near to you; it is in your mouth and in your heart for you to observe." (Deut. 30: 12-14)

Last Sunday as I drove in to church, I was listening again to Jim Gilbert, his 'nature notes" on WCCO. Those who listen to Jim know him to be a keen observer of the wonders of nature. But Jim also has other observers out there in the Minnesota northland who are watching with him. On Sundays they often call in to tell him what they've seen or observed, as the seasons come and go in this beautiful part of the world.

That Sunday there were listeners who called in to tell him about their first tomatoes. There was another who wanted to know what kind of nocturnal creature might be building a nest in his windowpane. He would clean it out during the day, but then each morning the remnants were there again. But there was one caller who had called in from Lake Mille Lacs with an observation that still haunts me today. He created an image that continues to rattle around inside my brain.

He had seen a baby loon, he said, swimming around the bay, and he was following not one of his own, but a drake mallard duck, near the cabin where he lived. It seems that some kind of strange adoption had taken place there, on the waters of the bay, and I can almost see that hopeful look in the little loon's eyes, riveted as they must have been on that emerald head and golden beak that swam before him. For that little loon the duck had become, as it were, the promised messiah, who could deliver him from whatever violence had taken his parents away.

Jim Gilbert himself was moved at this extraordinary twist in nature's plan. He hoped against hope that this little one would soon find one of his own to adopt him, for ducks are vegetarians, and loons are fish eater. The future seemed dim for that little guy unless he found one of his own.

It's a powerful image for me. A male duck was being asked to be a mother to another who wasn't even her kind.

How many little lost loons there are in the world! The children, bless them, whose parents have lost their way! (And bless them too!)   How many, indeed, who are looking for a home, for a "savior" as it were, who will lead them to a place of safety, protect them from the wicked weeds that grow at will?

I thank God for adoptive parents. I thank God for people who watch out for the little ones. People, who are willing to lift their wings, and calm the pounding hearts that come to them. I thank God for people who welcome the distressed, who love them, believe in them, and believe that this is how the world should be, people watching out for each other, regardless of the color of their feathers or their dietary choices.

"The Word is very near to you," our Scriptures tell us. Watch, and listen for the Word. It may be, in fact, paddling in the bay, just outside your window.

Prayer: Use our lives, O God, to touch the world with love. Stir us by your Spirit to be neighbors to those in need, and to welcome little ones of every age and color, serving them with willing hearts. In Jesus Name. Amen.

Living Christ in Our Lives

Scripture: Matthew 25:40 "Truly I tell you, just as you did it to one of the least of these who are members of my family, you did it to me."

Not long ago, in a little less than a two week period, the world lost a little of its soul.

One part was a princess, the other was a sister. Yet both were both, a sister and a princess wrapped in one.

You know whom I mean, of course. The one was Princess Diana of England and the other was Mother Teresa of Calcutta. One died young, and the other in her later years.

As I was thinking about these great losses to our world, I spotted the title of a book that sits on my shelf. I'm not even sure if I have ever read the book but I know I've always liked the title. *If You Want to Walk on the Water*, the title reads, *You've Got to Get Out of the Boat*. The princess and the sister were not afraid to leave the boat.

The world was greatly moved by the death of them both.

What was it about the Princess that captured our hearts? "What is all this fuss?" I asked myself. There were people in the news that I was convinced had for the most part only cared about themselves, who were trembling with tears when they heard of her death.

She certainly wasn't a perfect princess. The road she walked wasn't always straight and narrow. She would be the first to say, no doubt, that she had made a lot of mistakes along the way. Yet after the tragedy of her death, her life story dominated the daily news. Millions waited for several hours just to pay their last respects. Men and women alike openly expressed their grief for her, people from all over the world.

What was it about her that captured our hearts? There was her smile, of course. Her radiance. Her captivating beauty. Her presence. Her graciousness. And, there was her spunk, admired by young and old.

Everyone admired her heart. She was able to be the kind of person who seemed to be like one of us. She who was a "princess," seemed to also be a commoner. She, who was of royalty, we all believed, shared our sorrows and our joys.

She gave herself to the cause of those who were so often the shame of so many, the victims of AIDS, many of whom had been disowned by their own families. She touched the heart of things, and the inner spirits of the world who watched her.

Though different in so many ways, she and Mother Teresa were alike in that. Everyone admired their heart. They both cared deeply for those who were unloved, and for those who weren't so lovely. They sought to touch the "untouchables of life" and did.

When she stood before the audience to receive another of her many honors and public recognition, Mother Teresa once said, "I am a little pencil in the hand of a writing God who is sending a love letter to the world." Coming from anyone else that would probably have sounded phony. Coming from Mother Teresa, we knew it was real. She asked that the money from her Nobel Peace Prize be given to the poor. The words of her lips were in tune with the music of her life.

If You Want to Walk on Water the title glared at me, *You've Got to Get Out of the Boat.* Princess Diana and Mother Teresa were not afraid to get out of the boat. They rolled up their sleeves; then plunged in.

There is a marvelous story about a man who stood before God, his heart breaking from the pain and injustice of the world. "Dear God," he cried out, "look at all the suffering, the anguish and distress in the world. Why don't you send help?"

God responded. "I did send help. I sent you."

Mother Terese and Princess Diana believed that they had been sent. That's why now, now that they are dead, the world has lost a little of its soul. Yet think just how much soul the world could gain, if in each of us, their good would live on!   .

Prayer: Lord, make me an instrument of your peace. Help me to see that I, too, can be a "little pencil in the hand of a writing God," sending a love letter to the world. Thank you for all of those who have gone before us, to show us the way, especially our Lord, Jesus Christ, in whose name we pray. Amen.

The Day of St. Peter and St. Paul

Scripture: I Corinthians 3:16-17 "Do you not know that you are God's temple and that God's spirit dwells in you?"

June 29th is a special day in our Church Year. It is a specific day, each year, set aside to honor two of the giants of the Church's history. Their names are Peter and Paul. Today we call them saints so that the world will know that these two men have been the reason that millions have come to know and worship Jesus Christ.

Were they perfect? If we mean by that question were they without sin, of course not. But they were able to accomplish and fulfill that to which God had called them. In that sense they had achieved perfection, to be sure. Somehow, St. Paul and St. Peter, these two powerful figures of Jesus' day, were able to understand that they were God's holy temple, and realize that God's Spirit lived within them.

Consider Peter, if you will. A blustery, sunburned, fisherman who heard the call of Jesus and dropped everything to follow him. He was impetuous and rash. He was quick to leap, yet somehow reluctant and afraid to follow through. In his confession we see him bold, gutsy, and courageous, unafraid to take a stand, a leap of faith. Yet at the time of Jesus' trial we see him weak and impotent, three times denying the very One who changed his life.

Despite all of Peter's failings, his faith has become for us an inspiration. Following Jesus' death and resurrection, he became a powerful and persuasive evangelist for the Lord whom he had failed. He was the one to whom others looked for leadership and strength. Tradition tells us that at the end of his own life, Peter stood his ground, and that he too was crucified for the sake of his convictions. We are told that he humbly requested to be crucified upside down, so as not to be made equal with Jesus, his Master, in any way.

Consider Paul, if you will. We are told according to one of the books that was not included in our New Testament canon, the "Acts of Paul and Thecla," that he wasn't much to look at. Bald headed, bow legged, a strongly built man, small in size; with meeting eyebrows, and a rather large nose. His letters were strong, we were told by someone who had seen him, but his bodily presence was weak. Paul started out as an archenemy of the church, until one day he was knocked flat by a blaze of light that changed his life forever. As Fredrick Beuchner describes him, "Little by little the forgiven person became a forgiving person, the person who found he was loved became capable of love, the slob that God had faith in anyway, became de-slobbed, faithful, and good works blossomed from his branches, like fruit from a well watered tree." The letters that he wrote comprise a majority of the New Testament that we know and read today.

Writes Dale Turner:

"Centuries ago, Confucius spoke words that deserve to be heard in every century: "Seek not every quality in one individual." Will Rogers said it for our century, "We are all ignorant, only in different ways, and no one is as ignorant as an educated man outside his own field."

Even the greats had their imperfections. William Butler Yeats and George Bernard Shaw were poor spellers. Benjamin Franklin, Pablo Picasso and Carl Jung all had trouble with mathematics. One of Albert Einstein's teachers called him mentally slow, and Isaac Watts was called dull and inept by his teachers.

But God has a purpose for each of us, and there are times, sometimes too many times, when we forget that, and when we lose sight of how holy we are in God's sight. Emerson once wrote of the mountain that chided the squirrel because the squirrel was so small and insignificant. "Maybe so" responded the squirrel, "but if I cannot carry forests on my back, neither can you crack a nut."

Jesus believed that there were extraordinary powers that could be expressed through ordinary people. St. Peter and St. Paul are two of those. They, and others like them, who came from humble beginnings, turned the world upside down with a message of love and redemption.

Perhaps you remember as I do, a little poem by an unknown author, that says it in another way:

If you can't be a pine on the top of a hill,
Be a scrub in the valley, but be
The best little scrub on the side of the hill.
Be a bush, if you can't be a tree.
If you can't be a bush, be
A bit of the grass
And some highway happier make.
If you can't be a musky, then
Just be a bass,
But be the liveliest bass in the lake.
We can't all be captains; we've got to be crew,
There's something for all of us here.
There's big work to do and
There's lesser work, too,
And the thing we must do is
The near.
If you can't be a highway, then just
Be a trail.
If you can't be the sun, be a star.
It isn't by size that you
Win or you fail,
Be the best of whatever you are. (Anonymous)

Prayer: Today we give you thanks, O Lord, for St. Peter and Paul, two of the giants of faith that have gone before us to pave the way. Help us to capture the vision of that gift that you have given us, and of that person that you have called us to be. Help us to know that we too are your temples, and that your Spirit dwells within. In the name of Christ we pray. Amen.

A Prayer for Our Country

Fourth of July

Scripture: John 8:36: "So if the Son makes you free, you will be free indeed."

The 4th of July...what does it mean to you? Sometimes I think in our attempts to squeeze four-day weekends out of our national holidays, we lose sight of what these holidays are all about. Two hundred fourteen years ago our forefathers signed the Declaration of Independence. A new nation was conceived in the hearts and minds of people.

On days like today we are filled with pride. Nostalgia sweeps over us. We remember the "land where our father's died, and the land of the pilgrim's pride. We sing "America the Beautiful" with a lump in our throats, and we're reminded of what a gift it is to live in the kind of country that we do.

Some of you have traveled the world over, and you have experienced every kind of government there is and you have tasted the wonders of other nations, but few of you would ever trade this land for those. We are indeed among the blessed to live here.

Yet, at the same time, we are painfully aware of our problems as a nation. We are aware of the violence that stalks our nation and our culture. We are aware of the loneliness of people who live here, and the stark poverty that lives alongside lavish wealth. We are aware of the injustices of our economy, and of the blight of racism and prejudice that persists all around us. We are painfully aware of the suffering of our children, who seem to be more and more confused, and less and less secure. We are also aware of the frightening dependence of so many of our people on drugs, alcohol and gambling. We are aware of how easy it is to turn to war and more violence as the answer to our problems. As we breathe in the air of our cities, and see the smog that hovers over them, we are all too aware of the terrible blows that our greed has caused upon the earth, the sky, and water. Unless we cover our eyes with blinders, we know that our nation is far from perfect.

On July 4th, 1880, the great preacher Phillips Brooks, preaching in Westminster Abbey Cathedral in London, shared the following words:

"It is not for me to glorify the country which I love with all my heart and soul.

I may not ask your praise for anything admirable which the United States has been or done. But on my country's birthday I may do something far more solemn and more worthy of the hour. I may ask for your prayers in her behalf..."

And so do I ask, fellow travelers, for your prayers this morning, on our country's behalf:

Let us Pray: That we may learn to build not just buildings, but the inner souls of men and women.

That we may learn not just the mysteries of physics and of outer space, but the secrets of how it is that we can live together.

That as a nation, we may find the peace and love we need to feel good about ourselves.

That we are given the wisdom we need to deal with the terrible complexities that now surround us.

That we may learn to care enough, and give enough, so that all the people of our nation and our world will have enough, to live without the pain of hunger.

That Christ will lead us in our freedom here, in these United States. This is our prayer, today and always. Amen."

We're All in This Together

Scripture: Matthew 5:14-15 "You are the light of the world. A city built on a hill cannot be hid. No one after lighting a lamp puts it under the bushel basket, but on the lamp stand, and it gives light to the whole house."

The Pastor stood on the grassy hillside, like Jesus, in the afternoon sun. Gathered around him were twenty-five people who had chosen to volunteer to help clean up after the flood of '97. This was the "flood of floods." It struck the Red River Valley with a legendary vengeance. This was Grand Forks, North Dakota, a city that found itself in the heart of it all.

"You have chosen to enter our lives," the pastor said, "or else I would not show you this."

He pointed to the houses below. "That two story house there," he said, "was lifted completely off its foundation. You can see the water line there, just below the rooftop. These homes were completely under water. They are totally destroyed. Down the block a ways," he continued, "there is a garage that sits beside a house that didn't have a garage before. All of these homes have been condemned because of the flood's contamination."

"These were homes," he said, "that since the dike was built at 50 feet in the 1970's had never seen a drop of water, even in their basements. This year they were totally under water. The people who lived there are members of our congregation. She is a teacher. He is a salesman. They have two little children. They have no idea what they will do, or where they will go."

"We don't have funerals for houses," he said, "but we will have a service of closure for our families who lived there. Because the inside is contaminated, we will gather out in the yard. We will ask these families to visualize each of the rooms of the house in their mind. We will ask them to enter the memories of each of the rooms of their home, the things that were there, the things that happened there, and what they meant to them."

"Then we'll ask God to help them let go of the things, but to hold on to the memories, and bless them."

He talked about the stages of loss that people experience at times like this, the shock, the denial, the anger, the guilt, and hopefully the acceptance that can one day occur, through the healing of God and time. His voice quaked as he shared his pain with us, and the pain of his people. Tears filled his eyes.

As we walked along the avenue and saw pile after pile of junk, of damaged walls and doors stacked outside each home, we could only get a small glimpse at what all of this might mean.

Being there, in Grand Forks, in those days following the flood of '97, was overwhelming for me, and for those with whom I traveled. It was painful, powerful, rich, and spiritual all at the same time. We saw small symbols of hope. Stores reopened. Children played. A man mowed his lawn beside a house that would have to be leveled. He mowed his lawn, and planted flowers, nonetheless. The waters were beginning to recede. Yet make no mistake, the devastation had cast an ugly shadow over the city, like a pall.

The people called us "angels" as we worked beside them to clean up the mess. In those days that followed the flood, I learned once more that givers are the greatest receivers. Grace touched my soul in Grand Forks, North Dakota, in a strange and special way.

Writes Beuchner, "So our happiness is all mixed up with each other's happiness and our peace with each other's peace. Our own happiness, our own peace, can never be complete until we find some way of sharing it with people who, the way things are now, have no happiness and know no peace."

Jesus invites us to let our lights shine. We are encouraged to be life-givers to others and to love each other. For where love is, hope is never far behind.

Prayer: We are one family in you, O Christ. You have called us to give of ourselves in the midst of a world in which our own happiness and peace can never be complete until we find some way of sharing it with others. Help us to find the way, O God, so that we too may be fulfilled. In Jesus Name. Amen.

A God for the Inside and the Outside

Scripture: Psalm 139:7 "Where can I go from your spirit, where can I flee from your presence?"

We were spreading sealant on the basement walls of a home in Grand Forks, North Dakota. The fumes were beginning to bother me, so I decided to take a break. I grabbed a cup of coffee and strolled outside, down the sidewalk, to the back of the alleyway. Here is where all the backyards of this neighborhood come together.

It had been four months now since the then raging, now meek meandering Red River had overflowed its dikes. Millions and millions of dollars of damage and hundreds of heartaches were left behind.

As I stood looking thoughtfully down the alleyway, it occurred to me that if you were coming here for the first time today, you wouldn't even know the flood had happened. A bunny rabbit scampered in the grass, nibbling at the tender blades. A robin hopped along the alleyway and checked the puddle for some worms. The rhubarb was lush and green, and ready to be picked. The trees were waving in the summer breeze, the grass was thick and ready to be cut, the homes seemed scrubbed, the hedges trimmed, the flowers blooming.

On the outside, everything seemed fine. You would hardly know that in April these same yards looked like war zones.

But on the inside, in the basement, the story of the flood still lingered on. Furnaces were destroyed. Electrical wiring was disconnected, waiting to be redone from top to bottom. There were piles of things, everywhere. There was no place to walk, to sit down, to sleep, with just a narrow walkway in between the piles.

The family of three that we were there to help was literally in chaos. They had been told they had two hours to save what they could and get out of town. He, a Viet Nam vet, had had a flashback the day when the television helicopters came buzzing in to take their shots for the evening news. His stepson had a nervous breakdown, unable to cope with the losses of family heirloom left by his grandparents.

Across the river, we were told, there was a Lutheran church that you wouldn't even know had been touched by the water if you drove by it today. On the outside, it looked solid, stable, stretching its beautiful spire into the sky. On the inside, in the six-foot crawl space underneath the building, all of the electrical wires and heating ducts were totally ruined. The "guts" of the church had been ravaged. It would take thousands and thousands of dollars to restore the mechanicals and have them running again.

As I stood there, I realized how much that city in the valley seemed to be like you and I.

On the outside, we clean up very nicely, most of the time. But on the inside, there are the dreams that haunt us in the night, the piles of junk, the hidden fears, and the failures that we harbor. We can be coiffured, manicured, pedicured and self-assured—on the outside—but on the inside, in our six-foot crawl space, we can be feeling very much alone, just hoping to hang on.

That's why we needed to be there that day. We need to be there for each other. We need to be there in love, no matter what's on the outside or the inside. Jesus calls us there.

Prayer: Be with us, O Lord, as we live our outside lives, as well as our inside lives. Help us to know that You are always there, wherever we may be. In Jesus Name. Amen.

Children of the Heavenly Father

Scripture: Romans 8:14 "For all who are led by the Spirit of God, are children of God."

Sometime ago, when our granddaughter,Emily, was three, my wife, Joan, went down to help our daughter out with the children while she was involved in school conferences.

After Joan had been there for a while, she realized that the previous Sunday had been Emily's first Sunday in Sunday School.

"Emily" she said. "How was Sunday School?" But Emily said nothing; instead, she stood thoughtfully looking into space.

"What was your teacher's name?" her Grandma asked. "Do you remember?"

"Child of God," said Emily.

"What did you say?" asked Joan.

"Child of God," said Emily, looking just as serious as a three year old can look.

"Oh," said Grandma. "Did she have another name?"

"Sandy, child of God," said Emily.

It was then that my daughter chimed in. "We're all children of God, aren't we honey?"

And Emily thoughtfully nodded her head, without a smile.

What's your name? Sandy? John? Clarence? Eleanor? Mary Jane?

In our Baptisms we were all given a brand new name, "Child of God." Mary Jane...child of God. Terry....child of God. John....child of God.

These are words to live by. They are also words to die by. There are no greater words in all the world.

What they mean is that no matter where our lives will take us, no matter where we've been, or from where we're coming back, our name will always be the same.

"Child of God."

Prayer: Thank you, Heavenly Father, for the gift of Holy Baptism, and for calling us by name. Thank you for giving us a family and a home, that goes beyond our earthly home and family. Thank you for the promise that You are there for us forever, We are your children, Heavenly Father. You have called us to be Your own, and we are grateful. We pray in Jesus name. Amen.

The Blessings that are Right Beside Us

Scripture: John 6:68 "Simon Peter answered him, "Lord, to whom can we go? You have the words of eternal life."

In *Lutheran Book of Worship* there is a response that's sung by the congregation after the Second Lesson has been read that goes like this: "Alleluia, Lord to whom shall we go? You have the words of eternal life. Alleluia. Alleluia."

They are Peter's words, of course, from the Gospel reading for the 11th Sunday After Pentecost. Many of Jesus followers had begun to leave him. They had become disenchanted with some of his sayings, according to John. Because so many of them had turned back, Jesus turned to his Twelve Disciples and asked: "Do you also wish to go away?" Then came Peter's words. "Lord, to whom shall we go? You have the words to eternal life."

There are many of us who are like those early followers of Jesus. We too, quickly become disillusioned with Jesus. For many different reasons, we have walked away and left him. Some of us are looking for someone or something better to come along. There are those who are like me, who are always expecting that the "best is yet to come," so we are always looking around the next corner, or the next chapter of our lives, hoping to discover what we're looking for. We are hoping that at last we will discover who we really are, and who we were meant to be.

That was how it was with Nora Wimberly:

There is an old story that the wanderer, the seeker, frequently finds the illusive dream in his or her own backyard. I did. But like the wanderer, the journey toward discovery took years....

Finally, after years of looking fine on the outside, and feeling like a fraud on the inside, I had to let go of all my former notions of home. Finally, the motto I kept on my desk became reality. *We are not at home where we live, but where we are loved and understood.*

Finally, I began to meet the eternal Emmanuel—God with us, God with me; finally, I experienced a resurrection—from the inside out; finally, the Holy Spirit found a home in me—not just on the pages of a well thumbed Bible. Finally, I came home to my own skin, to those around me, and to God who had been there all along.

Home is where I am loved and understood. I found my elusive dream in my husband's eyes and arms, in my children and grandson, in my work, in my relationships with friends, and with those who are also at home with God. It is my own place at supper—the one I'll prepare tonight and the one presided over by the risen Christ. It is the truth of peace that does defy all human understanding. Home is life and love here and forever.

"Will you too go away?" asked Jesus.

"Lord to whom shall we go?" Asked Peter. "You have the words to eternal life."

God had blessed Peter with incredible insight. Peter knew that he needed to go no further. Home was standing there, before him. Home was not a place, but a person, who loved and understood him.

My youngest daughter Amy shared this little thought with me, and I pass it on to you. It's called, "Take Time to Listen."

The little child whispered, 'God speak to me.'
And a meadowlark sang. But the child did not hear.

So the child yelled. 'God let me see you!'
And a star shone brightly. But the child did not notice.

And the child shouted. 'God give me a miracle!'
And a life was born. But the child did not know.

So the child cried out in despair, 'Touch me God,
And Let me know that you are there!'
Whereupon God reached down,
And touched the child.
But the child brushed the butterfly away
And walked away unknowingly.

Confucius once said: "Take time to listen. Oftentimes the things we seek are right underneath our noses. Don't miss out on your blessing because it isn't packaged the way you'd expect."

Prayer: Lord, you do have the words of eternal life. Help us to listen that we may hear them. Help us to see You, standing before us. You are there in the eyes of our wife or husband, our children, our friends and those who care for us. You are closer than we would ever dare to dream. Help us to find our "home" in You. In Jesus Name. Amen.

Loving Our Neighbors as Ourselves

Scripture: James 2:8 "You do well if you really fulfill the royal law according to the scripture, 'You shall love your neighbor as yourself.'"

The author of the epistle of James, in his second chapter, speaks of the distinctions that we often make between people. We make them especially between those who are rich, and those who are poor. He warns us not to play the game of "favoritism," for whatever reasons there may be. "You would do well," he encourages, "If you really fulfill the royal law according to the scripture, 'You shall love your neighbor as yourself.'"

How easy it is to play favorites in life! We often make distinctions on the basis of how much people might be like us or unlike us, and we are easily drawn to the former, rather than the latter. We are easily drawn as well to those who might be useful to us in the future. We tend to ignore those who may not be able to return our favors.

These prejudices run deep within our souls. They are passed on from generation to generation. Sometimes, in spite of our best intentions, they are biases based on color, creed, race, family backgrounds, wealth or the lack of it. The list could go on and on. Our prejudices are fueled by our fears, our lack of understanding and awareness, our jealousies.

My dad's sister, known to me as a child as Aunt Lanore, died several years ago. When she was dying, my parents and I went to be with her. She lived in the remote wilderness area in and around Island Lake, Manitoba, some three hundred miles northeast of Winnipeg, and a hundred miles from the nearest road. My aunt had gone there thirty years earlier to teach the Cree, and to begin an English speaking school in that Native

American community of the far north. It was there, in her dying days, as we sat around her bedside, that I discovered for the first time that we, too, the Morehouse family, were of Indian ancestry. Coursing through our veins was the blood of those who first lived in North America. Chills ran up and down my spine, as I sat there, and learned of my roots!

Ever since then I have been especially aware of the dark prejudices that so many of us seem to have toward our Native American brothers and sisters. Sweet, well-meaning, people, who would be the first to call themselves Christians, will suddenly launch out into hate-filled discourse, and derogatory stereotyping, about a people that most of them have never tried to meet or understand. These are the biases that are embedded in us all. They are often passed on early in our childhood.

Our middle daughter Shelly, whom I often feel might have been inspired by her Great Aunt Lanore, and who now lives in Alaska, shared with us the following story. It's a good reminder to us all. It happened on a British Airways flight from Johannesburg, South Africa.

A middle aged, well-off white South African woman, found herself sitting next to a black man. She immediately called the cabin crew attendant over to complain about the seating.

"What seems to be the problem, Madam?" asked the attendant.

"Can't you see?" she said. "You've sat me next to a Kaffir. I can't possibly sit next to this disgusting human. Find me another seat!"

"Please calm down, Madam." The stewardess replied. The flight is very full today, but I'll tell you what I'll do. I'll go and check to see if we have any seats available in club or first class."

The woman cocks a snooty look at the outraged black man beside her (Not to mention many of the neighboring passengers).

A few minutes later the stewardess returns with the good news, which she delivers to the lady, who cannot help but look at the people around her with a smug and self-satisfied grin.

"Madam, unfortunately, as I suspected, economy is full. I've spoken to the cabin services director, and club is also full. However, we do have one seat in first class."

Before the lady has a chance to answer, the stewardess continues, "It is most extraordinary to make this kind of an upgrade, however, and I had to get special permission from the captain. But, given the circumstances, the captain felt that it was outrageous that someone be forced to sit next to such an obnoxious person."

With which, she turned to the black man sitting next to the woman, and said, "So if you would like to get your things, sir, I have your seat ready for you..."

At which point, apparently, the neighboring passengers stood and gave a standing ovation while the black man walked up to the front of the plane.

This little saying remains on our refrigerator door: "People will forget what you said. People will forget what you did. But people will never forget how you made them feel."

Prayer: There is a royal law that you have given us, O God. Too readily, we forget, to "love our neighbors as ourselves." Love seems to leave us, for lots of reasons, even sometimes in spite of our best intentions. Forgive us. Help us to understand that your love plays no favorites, and that it's your desires that ours might be the same. In Jesus Name. Amen.

These Offerings that Are Ours

Scripture: 2 Corinthians 4: 7 "But we have this treasure in clay jars, so that it may be made clear that this extraordinary power belongs to God and does not come from us."

If you have been a regular listener to "Faith Alive", our weekly radio broadcast, then you've heard a few Emily stories. Perhaps you've heard far more than you have even wanted to.

But I would daresay that you haven't heard a lot of "Erik" stories. Erik John Madigan is Emily's little brother, and he was three last year. It's Erik John who has convinced me that there is a difference between raising boys and girls. I'm the father of three girls, so I have never had the privilege of raising a son. But when my first grandson came along, I was given a few peeks at just what those differences might be. Within a five-minute period of time, Erik can charm you, or throw a brick at you, and you never quite know which is coming next.

The other morning he was in his charming stage. His dad had gone off to work early, and his mother, our daughter, was hoping to get a couple of minutes of extra sleep. She rolled over and closed her eyes, enjoying the luxury of having her three children still in bed. She thought they were in bed. Erik, however, was not. He was in the kitchen, lovingly fixing his mother breakfast in bed!

It wasn't long before she heard the pitter patter of little bare feet in her bedroom. Then she heard his voice. "Prise mama!" he said.

She opened her eyes, and there was her breakfast. It was a heaping bowl of marshmallows! "Prise mama," he said again, with a great big grin that flashed his incredible dimples. Our daughter accepted his little surprise with gratitude.

When I envisioned our little guy standing beside his mother's bed with a heaping bowl of marshmallows, I was reminded of one of the writings of Gerhard Frost. The author wrote of something very similar from his own life's experience. It's a little piece he called, "Soggy Cereal and Tepid Tea".

When I remember that I am a parent, and think of God as Father, I recall a special breakfast brought to me in bed.

It was an elaborate menu; chilled burnt toast, with peanut butter; eggs, fried and chilled too; soggy cereal (the milk had been added too soon) and tepid tea. A horrendous mix.

When they stepped out for a moment to get something they'd forgotten (Heaven forbid!) my wife whispered. "You're going to have to eat this, I can't!" And so I did.

I didn't eat as a gourmet, for it wasn't gourmet cooking; I didn't even eat as a hungry man, for I wasn't hungry.

I ate it as a father because it was made for me; I was expected to; they had faith in me. And I ate it because it was served on eager feet with starry eyes.

I think of my poor service to God as teacher, parent, interpreter of the Good News.

I know that my offerings are soggy, tepid, and unfit, but my Father receives them and even blesses them—not because I am good but because He is!

Prayer: Thank you, dear Lord, for accepting the gifts we offer to you, however soggy, tepid, or meager they are. Thank you for your patience with us. Thank you for your understanding and your love as we seek to be your children. Help us to know your goodness, so that we may willingly accept the gifts of others, imperfect though they be. Help us to see they are offered in love, and that they come, like a heaping bowl of marshmallows, to surprise us on our way. We pray in Jesus name. Amen.

It's All About Others

Scripture: Mark 8: 34-35 "He called the crowd with his disciples, and said to them, 'If any want to become my followers, let them deny themselves and take up their Cross and follow me. For those who want to save their life will lose it, and those who lose their life for my sake, and for the sake of the gospel will save it."

How terribly strange the words of Jesus sound to modern ears today! The words of Jesus tremble with dissonance and discord in a day and age that seems determined to perpetuate the conviction that "it's really all about me." "I want to have my needs met. If my needs aren't being met, then I'm out of here," people seem to say not only with their words, but by their actions.

So relationships are frequently abandoned with very little effort to make them work. Lawsuits abound because someone didn't get their way. Children grow up in single parent homes with very little contact from a father or a mother who gave them birth.

It's all about me.

It seems that Jesus was well aware of the destructive nature on this "all about me" mentality. He warned his followers that they must first deny themselves if they wish to be counted as true disciples. He understood that oftentimes the only thing that stands between God and me is I. Every time I try to walk alone, I trip over myself.

Charles Allen shares with us the following:

In Hiawatha, Kansas, in the Mt. Hope Cemetery, stands a strange group of gravestones.

A guy named Davis, a farmer, and a self-made man,

had them erected. He began as a lowly hired hand, and by sheer determination and frugality he managed to amass a considerable fortune in his lifetime. In the process, however, the farmer did not make many friends. Nor was he close to his wife's family, since they thought she had married beneath her dignity. Embittered, he vowed never to leave his in-laws a thin dime.

When his wife died, Davis erected an elaborate statue in her memory. He hired a sculptor to design a monument which showed both her and him at opposite ends of a love seat. He was so pleased with the result, that he commissioned another statue—this time of himself, kneeling at her grave, placing a wreath on it. That impressed him so greatly that he planned a third monument, this time of his wife kneeling at his future gravesite, depositing a wreath. He had the sculptor add a pair of wings on her back, since she was no longer alive, giving her the appearance of an angel. One idea led to another until he'd spent no less than a quarter million dollars on the monuments to himself and to his wife! Whenever someone from the town would suggest he might be interested in a community project (a hospital, a park and swimming pool for the children, a municipal building, etc.) the old miser would frown, set his jaw, and shout back, "What's this town ever done for me? I don't owe this town nothing'."

After using up all his resources on stone statues and selfish pursuits, John Davis died at 92, a grim faced resident of the poorhouse. But as to his monuments, it's strange. Each one is slowly sinking into the Kansas soil, fast becoming victims of time, vandalism, and neglect. Monuments of spite. Sad reminders of a self-centered unsympathetic life. There is a certain poetic justice in the fact that within a few years, they will be gone.

Oh, by the way, very many people attended Mr. Davis' funeral. It is reported that only one person seemed genuinely moved by any sense of personal loss. He was Horace England, the tombstone salesman.

Contrast John Davis' story with that of Mary Jo Copeland of Minneapolis, Minnesota. At most homeless shelters, new arrivals are given the basics: a cot, a blanket and a plain hot meal. Mary Jo Copeland believes that is not enough. At her charity, this 5'6" dynamo doesn't give her clients a pat on the back or even a gentle caress on the cheek.

She gets down on her knees and washes their feet.

In a hard-knock world, that simple gesture of compassion is enough to bring tears to the eyes of some of the most hardened of hearts that enter her place. "Nobody every did this for me," says Wayne Irving a homeless laborer from Chicago who arrived in Minneapolis by bus. Sitting over a basin of hot sudsy water, Copeland, age 57, wearing a thick pair of rubber surgical gloves, rubs his callused feet with antiseptic ointment. "I've never met anyone like her in my life."

That's because there aren't many men and women like Copeland. With little more than a card table and a couple of coffeepots, she founded a storefront charity 14 years ago on the edge of downtown Minneapolis. Today she is the guiding light of "Sharing and Caring Hands", a three million dollar nonprofit community center that caters daily to as many as 1,800 of the city's needy, dispensing everything from hot heals and bus tokens to eyeglasses and deodorant. "It's heartwarming to see thousands of people benefit," says Jim Ramstad, congressman and sometime volunteer. "Nobody does more to help people in need. Mary Jo is a true saint...Minnesota's Mother Teresa."

Copland, who draws no salary, says her work springs from a biblical mandate. "I believe in what Jesus said about helping the less fortunate in memory of him," she says. "That's why I wash their feet. We are commanded to be servants of the poor."

Mary Jo lives the words of our scripture lesson today. John Davis probably never heard them, at least not so that he took them to heart.

Prayer: O God, deliver us from ourselves, from our selfishness, and our sin. Help us to bend our knees and our hearts, and not be afraid to stretch out our arms towards others. Help us to learn that it's not just about us. It's about You, and your kingdom coming to us. In Jesus Name. Amen.

Simply Out of This World

Scripture: John 18:33 "Then Pilate entered the headquarters again, summoned Jesus, and asked him, "Are you the King of the Jews?""

The scene that our Gospel creates in our minds today is simply out of this world. It's like a story we read or a dream that we had, that couldn't be true. Yet it seemed so true that it still sends shivers up and down our spine.

Jesus…beaten, bruised, battered, and still bleeding from his lashing in the courtyard square, standing before the governor of the land, the most powerful person in all of Judea. Jesus is standing there, with one eye swollen shut, sweating, and smelling of the streets; the governor asks him, "Are you the King of the Jews?"

It must be all that Pilate can do to keep from laughing as he asks that question. But he asks it anyway. "Are you the King of the Jews?"

"My kingdom," said Jesus, "is not from this world. My kingdom is not from here."

What did he mean, I wonder? And what does it mean to say, "Christ is King" and to worship him this Sunday morning that has been given that name? What does it mean to pray as we do each Sunday in the prayer that he taught us to pray, "Thy Kingdom Come, Thy Will Be Done?"

In my earlier years of ministry, when I served our church at Waconia, we had a delightful little German man with a twinkle in his eye and a warm and welcome smile that we hired as our church custodian. Leander was his name. "Leander Schlumpberger" to be exact. He was looking for a part time job to supplement his Social Security income, and I can see him clearly in my mind even now. I quickly learned that Leander would be sharing with me and the other members of the church the wisdom of his years.

In our interview, I asked Leander where he was from. He told me that he had been born and raised in New Ulm, Minnesota. Naturally I wanted to impress him with my knowledge of the world, and that I happened to know a little bit about New Ulm, Minnesota, so I said, "Isn't that the home of Hauenstein Breweries?" (Great question for a pastor to be asking, don't you think?) Well, I don't think that Leander was very impressed, but he patiently explained to me that it used to be the home of Hauenstein beer, but no longer. It had been sold, he said, and became a part of Hamm's.

Leander went on to tell that he had known the Hauenstein family when he was growing up. He had gone to school with them and at one point lived across the street from one of the children. "He was the last of the family," Leander said, "and the president of the company. But he couldn't live with prosperity. He had all these things, and everything he wanted had been handed to him. And then one morning he walked into his office, took out a gun, and blew his own head off."

"He couldn't live with prosperity," he said. Deep inside he was a lonely and tormented man, who hurt so badly, that he chose to end it all.

"My kingdom is not of this world," said Jesus, as he stood there with his bruised and battered face and body before one of the most powerful men in the land. Pontius Pilate must have wondered what in the world he meant by that.

A friend of mine shared with me an anonymous little piece that someone had written that was simply called, "The Paradox".

The paradox of our time in history is that we have taller buildings, but shorter tempers; wider freeways, but narrower viewpoints.

We spend more, but have less; we buy more but enjoy it less.

We have bigger houses and smaller families; More conveniences but less time.

We have multiplied our possessions, but reduced our values.

We talk more, love too seldom, and hate too often.

We've learned how to make a living, but not a life.

We've added years to life, not life to years.

We've been all the way to the moon and back; But have trouble crossing the street to meet our neighbors.

These are the days of two incomes, but more divorce. Of fancier houses, but broken homes.

We've conquered outer, but not inner space."

That sounds like a pretty negative commentary, to be sure. But it seems to be true that we may be the victims of our own good times. The real price of our prosperity may be in how hard it has become to see beyond it.

And so we hear again his soft but insistent voice,\ as he stands there in the governor's hall. "My kingdom is not of this world".

Prayer: Help us ,O Lord, to look deeply into the promises of this world, and to discover instead the treasures of your kingdom. Help us to know the deep and lasting joy that comes from giving ourselves to others in love, even as you have given yourself to us. In Jesus name. Amen.

Honor Your Father and Mother

Scripture: I John 5:2 "By this we know that we love the children of God, when we love God and obey his commandments."

Once there was an old man who had lost his wife and lived alone. He had worked hard as a tailor all his life, but misfortunes had left him penniless, and now he was so old he could no longer work for himself. His hands trembled too much to thread a needle, and his vision blurred too much for him to make a straight stitch. He had three sons, but they were all grown and married now, and they were so busy with their own lives, they had only time to stop by and eat dinner with their father once a week.

Gradually the old man grew more and more feeble, and his sons all came by to see him less and less. "They don't want to be around me at all now," he told himself, "because they're afraid that I'll become a burden." He stayed up all night worrying what would become of him, until at last he thought of a plan.

The next morning he went to his friend the carpenter, and asked him to make a large chest. Then he went to see his friend the locksmith, and asked him to give him an old lock. Finally he went to see his friend the glassblower, and asked for all the old broken pieces of glass he had.

The old man took the chest home, filled it to the top with the broken glass, locked it up tight, and put it beneath his kitchen table. The next time his sons came for dinner, they bumped their feet up against it.

"What's in the chest?" they asked, looking under the table.

"Oh, nothing" the old man replied, "Just some things I've been saving."

His sons nudged it and saw how heavy it was. They kicked it and heard it rattling inside. "It must be full of all the gold he's saved over the years," they whispered to one another.

So they talked it over and realized they needed to guard the treasure. They decided to take turns living with the old man, and that way they could look after him too. So the first week the youngest son moved in with his father, and cared and cooked for him. The next week the middle son took his place, and the week after the eldest son took a turn. This went on for some time.

At last the old father grew sick and died. The sons gave him a very nice funeral, for they knew that there was a fortune sitting beneath the kitchen table, and they could afford to splurge a little on the old man now.

When the service was over, they hunted through the house until they found the key, and unlocked the chest. And of course, they found it full of broken glass.

"What a rotten trick!" yelled the eldest son. "What a cruel thing to do to your own sons!"

"But what else could he have done, really?" asked the middle son, sadly. "We must be honest with ourselves. If it wasn't for this chest, we would have neglected him until the end of the days."

"I'm so ashamed of myself," sobbed the youngest. "We forced our own father to stoop to deceit, because we would not observe the very commandment he taught us when we were young."

"But the eldest son tipped the chest over to make sure there was nothing valuable hidden among the glass after all. He poured broken pieces onto the floor, until it was empty. Then the three brothers silently stared inside, where they now read an inscription left for them on the bottom. "Honor Thy Father and Thy Mother." (From—*The Book of Virtues* by William Bennett)

"For the love of God is this," writes St. John. "That we obey his commandments. It's a story to remember, not just on Father's Day, but every day.

Prayer: So often we see your commandments, O God, as a list of "Thou Shalt nots" and nothing more. Gently remind us on this Father's Day, that they are instead the concrete, real life ways, that you have given us, to show us how to love You, and all of humankind. We pray in Jesus name. Amen.

Friends Don't Happen Every Day

Scripture: John 15:13 "No one has greater love than this, to lay down one's life for one's friends."

My good friend and colleague Pastor Jim Anderson was telling me about a wonderful luncheon that he had recently attended. He had been invited by an old friend who happened to be a well-known and creative author, a writer who has been an inspiration to many. His colorful and imaginative worship services, his hymns, and his devotional books continue to be admired throughout the church. When the guests had arrived, they learned that the reason that the five of them had been invited was because it was the author's 64th birthday. He had chosen to gather the five people who had "meant the most to him" throughout his life, and to thank them, as a part of this birthday celebration.

That's exactly what he did. He went around the table, one by one, and told each one why they had been included, how important they had been in his life, and why.

Can you imagine? As I thought about that luncheon, I couldn't help but imagine the tears that must have welled up in all of their eyes.

"Now why couldn't I have thought of something like that?" I mused to myself. Then I thought about the names that I would choose, and with their faces came a rush of gratitude and warmth.

"It was wonderful," said Pastor Anderson. "So humbling! I had no idea that my friendship had meant that much to him." His cup was literally "running over" for days after that luncheon.

Such is the essence of friendship. Oftentimes people who are there for us have no idea that they are doing anything out of the ordinary. They're just there because they want to be, have to be, and wouldn't choose to be anywhere else in the entire world.

How empty our lives would be without friends! They speak to us of God's love. They are God's love, in flesh and blood.

I was shopping not long ago at the grocery store in Moose Lake, Minnesota, near our summer cabin. My eyes were drawn to two young men in the checkout line next to mine. It was their appearance that got my attention. I could see the back of the head of one of them, which was completely shaved. There was a tattoo on the back of that shaved head that appeared to be shaped somewhat like the combination of a cross, a swastika, and the peace sign, all in one. "Ouch," I thought to myself, "that must have hurt." I began to wonder if his hair would ever grow back again if he would choose to let it. Being the old fuddy-duddy pastor that I am, I was trying to imagine him at his first job interview after high school or college. His ears were pierced. So were his eyelids. There were several rings dangling from the many orifices that were pierced on a variety of places on his body.

His friend stood by. He was huge! He wore a grubby black T-shirt and baggy pants. The kind that hung so low you were certain they would fall down any second? You know the look, don't you? His thick black hair looked as though it hadn't been washed in weeks, and lay in matted clumps with no real sense of order that I could see.

The boy with the tattoo said to the other, "My mom just never seems to like my friends. I don't know why." I couldn't help but chuckle. This could have easily been a cartoon in the morning paper! Perhaps God was reminding me that there is no prescription for what a friend should look like.

But I think that Rabbi Karen Kedar has some good advice for all of us, when she writes:

> The people
> In your life mirrors your world.
> If they are hollow, dull, or cruel,
> So will you see your life.

If they are loving, inspirational, and supportive,
You will reflect their beauty...

Choose your companions wisely,
Seek your teachers well,
Consider carefully the ones you engage
In serious conversation.

Look into the eyes of those who surround you,
And you will see a reflection of yourself.
(*God Whispers*)

Prayer: Thank you, Lord, for the friends who have lightened the way of our journey. For their wisdom, their honesty, spoken in love, their shoulders to cry on, for their laughter that warms our souls. Remind us, O Christ, that it isn't their outsides that matter. Help us to look into their eyes, and discover the completion of the person, we could never be without them. In Jesus name. Amen.

The Little Country Church

Scripture: Isaiah 6:1 "In the year that King Uzziah died, I saw the Lord, sitting on a throne, high and lofty; and the hem of his robe filled the temple."

L ike many Minnesotans, I have to spend a little time, "up north," as we like to say.

On an early, crisp summer morning bike ride, I saw the sign. "Faith Lutheran Church," it said, "7 miles West on County 46. Sunday School—9: 30 a.m. Worship—10: 30 a.m."

I hadn't really thought about it, until I read the sign. I assumed that I would worship that morning in town as I usually do when we're "up north." But why not Faith, I reasoned?

Why not Faith, indeed!

There were seven miles of countryside from the little town of Sturgeon Lake, Minnesota to Faith Lutheran Church. Dairy cows dotted the pastureland, and two pretty little rivers and a tiny country creek wound their way through the rugged farming country of the north. "This is northern rural America," I thought to myself, "and not an easy place to make a living."

Soon, I saw the church. It's little white frame building and silent steeple reached out to welcome me in a most unassuming way. Flooded with memories of early days in ministry, I drove into the parking lot, where I could count the cars and pick-up trucks and not use all of my fingers.

I zipped up the stairs at 10:29 a.m.—a habit my wife is still trying to break me of!—where I was greeted by the pastor at the door, with his robes draped over his arm, not yet dressed for worship. I took my place in the very last pew, as any good Lutheran would do. The pastor strolled casually down the center aisle; robes still drooped over his arm, greeting the faithful few who had made their worship on this Sunday morning in May. Garrison Keioller would love this place I decided. I had found Lake Woebegone at last!

In the morning announcements the pastor said, "Gladys? Do you want to say something about the lunch tomorrow after the parade?" You could almost feel Gladys gulp, and you could see her die inside. "There'll be a pot luck lunch after the service," she stammered. Gladys could easily have wrung the pastor's neck for asking.

The organ and the organist were old, and yet they persevered. They sang the good old hymns, "Holy, Holy, Holy" and "Father Most Holy." Twenty-five people in all lifted their lusty voices and sang their praise to God. Terry Johnson read the Word. He wore a short-sleeved shirt that morning. His ruddy cheeks betrayed the roughness of the wind and sun on those who spend time outdoors. He read the Word, and he read it well.

"In the year that King Uzziah died," he read. Once again we were whisked back in time to that great vision of the prophet Isaiah.

When the pastor preached that day he came out in front and said, "Since you're all sitting so far back this morning, I am coming down to you." So he did. He came right down that center aisle to the place where those scattered faithful few began, and there he stood and preached without a note in hand.

"This awesome God," he began. "Here we are, to worship Him again, exactly like Isaiah did in the 6th century before Christ in the temple of Israel."

"There aren't many of us here this morning" he continued. "Our church is small, and white, in the middle of the country. But you don't have to be in Westminster Cathedral or the Sistine Chapel in Rome to experience this awesome God." His sermon was simple, yet profound. He preached. We listened. He gave. The Spirit moved. And he was right. You don't have to be in the Sistine Chapel to experience this awesome God.

God was real to me that morning, in that little country church, where the Holstein cows grazed outside the window. It was about as different as night from day as I thought about my normal Sunday morning. But I was glad that I chose "Faith" that day. God comes to us, in awesome ways. Praise Him!

Prayer: You are an awesome God, O Lord! You often come to us in the least expected places of our lives, slipping in to bless us, unaware. Your voice is mostly soft and gentle in these places, but sure like Terry Johnson as he read the Word that day. Thank you, for faithful pastors, faithful churches, and your faithful people everywhere. Bless them as they gather to give you thanks and praise. In the Name of Christ we pray. Amen.

This Extravagant God

Scripture: Matthew 20:14 "Take what belongs to you, and go; I choose to give to this last the same as I give to you."

There is a parable that Jesus tells that seems to rankle most of us who read it. It jars our sense of justice, and of what is right, and of what is fair.

The problem is that Jesus tells us this story. And most of us have a pretty high regard for the stories Jesus tells, even though we don't always understand just what they mean. And we have an even higher regard for the life Jesus lived, and the death he died. That makes us want to listen closely to the words he has to say.

This particular parable from which our scripture lesson comes today has to do with a man who went out to hire laborers to work in his vineyard. He hired some of them early in the morning, and agreed with them how much they would be paid for their day of labor. Then he sent them off to work.

A little while later, he saw some others, standing idle in the marketplace, and he told them that they should go to work as well, and he would pay them what was right. And they did. That was about nine o'clock in the morning. About three o'clock he did the same.

At five o'clock, he went out again, and found some others who were just standing around, and he sent them off to work as well, and he promised them all, that he would pay them what was right.

When evening came, you remember the story, don't you? He gathered all of his workers together, and he paid them all the same. Those who had been hired early in the morning received exactly what they had been promised, but those who were hired later, at nine, at three, and at five received exactly the same as those who were hired at the crack of dawn!

The message of the parable seems to be about the way God keeps score. It's a lot different from the way we do. We seem to like to keep track, not only of the good that we do, but also of the mistakes that are made by others. We like to add those things up very carefully in columns, and we usually have it figured so that we are often ahead of the other person. Jesus story reminds us that God isn't in to counting games. God's mercy, God's love, slashes all of our previous conceptions. You could say that God uses a "new math" that we don't understand.

If you think about it all, that's good news. It means that you and I can get a fresh start each day. No matter what I've done or who I've been the day before, I can start all over again. None of us would want to be judged the way we so often judge others or paid the way we might pay them. Our parable reminds us of God's extravagant kindness.

I'm not sure whom the poet was who wrote these words, but he or she has given us some real food for thought:

The Wonder of It All

Suppose God charged us for the rain,
Or put a price on a songbird's strain
Of music, the dawn mist on the plain?
How much would autumn landscapes cost?
Or a window etched with winter's frost,
And the rainbow's glory, so quickly lost?

Suppose that people had to pay
To see the sunset's crimson play
And the magic stars on the Milky Way?
Suppose it was fifty cents a night
To watch the pale moon's silvery light,
Or watch a gull in graceful flight?

How much, I wonder, would it be worth
To smell the good, brown, fragrant earth
In Spring? The miracle of birth—
How much do you think people would pay
For a baby's laugh at the close of day?
Suppose God charged us for them I say;

Suppose we paid to look at the hills,
Or the rippling mountain rills,
Or the mating song of the Whippoorwills,
Or the curving breakers of the sea,
Or grace, and beauty, and majesty?

And all these things— my friends,
God gives us free!
The wonder of it all!

The story of the Bible is the story of God doing more....
more than his people would have dreamed, and far more than
they ever deserved. And that's the wonder of it. That's ours
through faith.

**Prayer: Thank you, Father, for your extravagant kindness.
Thank you, Jesus, for your never-failing love. Thank you, O
Spirit of this Living God, for your gifts, which are new every
day! In Your threefold name we pray, Father, Son, and Holy
Spirit. Amen.**

The Place with No Problems

Scripture: Romans 5:3-5 "And not only that, but we also boast in our sufferings, knowing that suffering produces endurance, and endurance produces character, and character produces hope, and hope does not disappoint us, because God's love has been poured into our hearts through the Holy Spirit that has been given to us."

I've always fancied myself as a realist. Not gloomy. But not a Pollyanna either. Someone called me an optimist after listening to one of my sermons the other day. It was a surprise to me. As I thought about it, I realised that Christians are optimists by nature of their faith.

The older I get, however, the more I'm aware of how powerful our attitudes are. They can make us, or break us, in so many ways.

I like to walk a lot. On these warm summer evenings, I often meet a lot of folks along the way. There are those who look down when they see that I am coming. I like to greet them anyway, just to see what they will do. Saying "hello" shouldn't be a major risk these days, but many seem to think it is.

Consider the family living down the block that I saw last night. They saw me coming then they walked away. They grabbed their kids. They shooed their dog. They ducked behind the tree. These are folks who've lived in my neighborhood just as long as we have. I don't even know their name.

On the other hand, there's Ray. He came out to the curb to greet me and called me by name. What a difference that can make! I walked away with a warm and peaceful feeling.

Or take that happy jogger I saw last night. Most joggers aren't very happy. Their exercise hurts too much, perhaps.

"Hi!" I said.

"How're you doing?" he asked.

"Great!" I said. "Beautiful night, isn't it?"

"Fantastic," he puffed. "It just doesn't get any better."

It was a little exchange. No big deal. Yet I smiled again as I walked away. It brightened my walk the rest of the way.

In one of the best selling volumes of *Chicken Soup for the Soul* Ken Blanchard shares with us one of the late Norman Vincent Peale's favorite stories:

> One day, I was walking down the street, when I saw my friend George approaching. It was evident from his downtrodden look that he wasn't overflowing with the ecstasy and exuberance of human existence, which is a high-class way of saying that George was dragging bottom.
>
> Naturally I asked him, "How are you George?" While that was meant to be a routine inquiry, George took me seriously and for fifteen minutes he enlightened me on how he had felt. The more he talked the worse I felt.
>
> Finally I said to him, "Well, George, I'm sorry to see you in such a depressed state. How did you get this way?" That really set him off.
>
> "It's my problems," he said. "Problems...nothing but problems. I'm fed up with problems. If you could get rid of all my problems I would contribute $5000 to your favorite charity."
>
> Well, now, I am never one to turn a deaf ear to such an offer, and so I meditated, ruminated, and cogitated on the proposition and came up with an answer that I thought was pretty good.
>
> I said, "Yesterday I went to a place where thousands of people reside. As far as I could determine, not one of them has any problems. Want to go there?"
>
> "When can we leave? That sounds like my kind of place," answered George.
>
> "If that's the case, George," I said, "I'll be happy to

take you tomorrow to Woodlawn Cemetery because the only people I know that don't have problems are dead."

Writes Blanchard. "I love that story. It really puts life in perspective. I heard Norman say many times, "If you have no problems at all, I warn you, you're in grave jeopardy—you're on the way out and you don't even know it! If you don't believe that you have any problems, I suggest that you immediately race from wherever you are, jump into your car and drive home as fast but as safely as possible, run into your house, and go straight to your bedroom and slam the door. Then get on your knees and pray, "What's the matter, Lord? Don't you trust me anymore? Give me some problems!"

What do you see as you're walking along? A sky full of blue? Or the encroaching clouds?

Prayer: Problems are a part of life, O God. Some of them are very serious, and not to be denied. Be with us in the midst of them, and give us the courage, and the hope that comes along with them. Help us to endure our sufferings, and be Your joyful presence wherever we can, as we begin our journey today. We pray in Jesus Name.

St. Francis of Assisi

Scripture: Psalm 19:3-4 "There is no speech, nor are there words; their voice is not heard; yet their voice goes out through all the earth, and their words to the end of the world."

"The Heavens are telling the glory of God," the Psalmist writes in Psalm 19, "and the firmament proclaims his handiwork. Day to day pours forth speech, and night to night declares knowledge. There is no speech, nor are their words; their voice is not heard; yet their voice goes out to all the earth, and their words to the end of the world." (19:1-4)

The Psalmist reminds us today of the "voiceless voice of heaven."

Perhaps no one heard that voice quite as clearly as the beloved St. Francis of Assisi. Our church has set aside October 4th for us to remember him.

There are countless stories about St. Francis and his love affair with God's creation and the creatures of God's kingdom. St. Francis never mistook the "creation" for the "Creator," for it was always God who breathed His breath of life and beauty into everything that had come to be.

Let me share with you today just one of those stories from the life of this beloved man of God. There are so many. James Baldwin tells this one:

"Very kind and loving was St. Francis—kind and loving not only to men, but to all living things. He spoke of the birds as his little brothers of the air, and he could never bear to see them harmed.

At Christmas time he scattered crumbs of bread under the trees so the tiny creatures could feast and be happy.

Once when a boy gave him a pair of doves that he had snared, St. Francis had a nest made for them, and the mother bird laid her eggs in it.

By and by, the eggs hatched and a nestful of young doves grew up. They were so tame that they sat on the shoulders of St. Francis and ate from his hand.

And many other stories are told of this man's great love and pity for the timid creatures that lived in the woods.

One day as he was walking among the trees the birds saw him and flew down to him. They sang their sweetest songs to show how much they loved him. Then, when they saw he was about to speak, they nestled softly in the grass and listened.

"O little birds" he said. "I love you, for you are my brothers and sisters of the air. Let me tell you something, my little brothers, my little sisters; You ought always to love God and praise him."

"And think of this, O little brothers; you sow not, neither do you reap, for God feeds you. He gives you the rivers and the brooks from which you drink. He gives you the mountains and the valleys where you may rest. He gives you the trees in which to build your nests."

"You toil not, neither do you spin, yet God takes care of you and your little ones. It must be, then, that he loves you. So do not be ungrateful, but sing his praises and thank him for his goodness toward you."

Then the saint stopped speaking and looked around him. All the birds sprang up joyfully. They spread their wings and opened their mouths to show they understood his words. And when he had blessed them, all began to sing; and the whole forest was filled with sweetness and joy because of their wonderful melodies." (*Book of Virtues*—William Bennet)

Prayer: For our little brothers and sisters of the air, God, we pray this day, and for our brother Francis whom we honor. You have touched our lives, O God, with the "voiceless voice of heaven" through the wonder of Your hand! We praise You, and glorify Your Name forever! Amen.

Singing a Song to the Darkness

Scripture: Colossians 3:16 "Let the word of Christ dwell in you richly; teach and admonish one another in all wisdom; and with gratitude in your hearts, sing psalms, hymns, and spiritual songs to God."

Not long ago I read about a thirteen-year-old girl, who had been in a coma for almost three months. She had passed the point of no return in terms of the hopes and dreams of friends and family. All at once this young girl began to respond, when her adopted horse was brought to her bedside and nuzzled her, as it were, back to life again. Now she is appearing on National Television Network broadcasts to tell her story, of how the nurturing of her horse had pulled her from the darkness of her coma, and urged her to carry on the story of her life.

Recently I heard another story sent shivers through my spine. Pastor G. Steve LaSalle tells the story of Karen, an active member of the Panther Springs United Methodist Church in Morristown, Tennessee.

When Karen was pregnant with her second child, a seemingly normal pregnancy, her 3-year-old son Michael began a relationship with his unborn sister by singing to her every night. Night after night, he would sing his new sister a song.

When it came time for Karen to give birth to her baby, there was trouble during the delivery. Michael's baby sister was in serious condition by the time she was finally born. The infant was immediately rushed to the neonatal intensive care unit at St. Mary's Hospital in Knoxville, Tennessee. As the days crawled by, the infant grew weaker. The pediatric specialist told the family it looked very grave for the little girl, and began to prepare them for the expected death.

During her stay in the intensive care unit, Michael asked continually about seeing his little sister. He wanted to sing to her. At the beginning of the second week, they dressed Michael in an oversized scrub suit and took him into the unit to see his sister. The medical personnel got angry because the three-year-old was in the unit. His mom protested, however, and said, "He is not leaving until he sings to his sister." Michael made his way over to the bassinet that held his sick little sister. He began to sing this song:

"You are my sunshine, my only sunshine, you make me happy, when skies are gray. You'll never know dear, how much I love you. Please don't take my sunshine away."

Woman's Day magazine called it the "miracle of a brother's song." The doctor just called it a miracle! Karen called it a miracle of God's love. The next day, when they thought they might be planning a funeral, they took Michael's sister home. She had responded immediately to the familiar voice of her brother.

God sings a song to us today, calling us from whatever darkness we may find ourselves in. He sings with a voice that was speaking to us, even before we were born.

And we are also called to sing God's song. We are urged to stand beside people in their pain, to sing the gentle song of life. Who are those who need to hear your song today? Could there be someone right in your family? Or maybe right next door?

Prayer: For the miracles of life and living, O God, of tenderness and gentle melodies of life, we give you thanks today. For sunshine songs, that echo through the corridors of time, and come to us, with life and love, we give you thanks and praise your holy name. Help us to be singers of the song! In Jesus Name. Amen.

When the Waters Are Up to Our Necks

Scripture: Psalm 69:1 "Save me, O God, for the waters have come up to my neck."

In a recent television documentary examining the unemployment problem in the United States, a reporter stuck a microphone in the face of a steelworker whose plant had just been closed. Not only his job, but also his entire community and his way of life had just been shattered. "How do you feel?" the reporter asked. The steelworker groaned, "I feel like I'm in a lake, and the water is up to my neck, and there's nothing I can do to stop it. I'm waiting for somebody with a life raft."

Compare his words, if you will, to the words of the Psalmist is Psalm 69.

> "Save me O God!
>> For the waters have come up to my neck.
>> I sink in deep mire
>> Where there is no foothold;
>> I have come into deep waters
>> And the flood sweeps over me.
>
> I am weary with my crying
>> My throat is parched
> My eyes grow dim
>> With waiting for my God."

The cameras of the evening news are always busy it seems. A sudden explosion on a flight to Paris, and suddenly the lives of the family and friends of all two hundred fifty people on board have been turned upside down.

I watched those families on the evening news. Many of them gathered by the sea to try to say goodbye to the ones they loved, but whose bodies they couldn't see. A woman and a man and a little girl embraced as the sea curled around their feet, and the relentless waves crashed in around them. Two little boys— was it their Dad I wondered who was on that plane?—planted roses in the sand, and scurried to the shore as a breaker rumbled in behind their feet.

"Save me O God!" the psalmist pleads, "for the waters have come up to my neck. My eyes grow dim with my waiting for my God."

We, too, find ourselves waiting, while the waters rise around us sometimes. We wait for the news that we already know is true. None of us chooses to be here, but once in a while that's where our travels lead us.

Where do we turn in times like these? The "Yellow Pages" has lists of professionals to whom we can turn. There are doctors and counselors, pastors and priests, psychologists and psychiatrists, many of whom are good and caring and skilled at helping in our times of crisis. However, some of them are quacks, and charlatans, eager to make a buck from someone else's pain. We can't always tell the "good guys" from the "bad guys" or those in between.

In the Psalmists' view of things, there was no feeling, no pain, no complaint, no angry moment that could not be entrusted to God. The Psalmists didn't believe that God would take away the painful realities of living. They simply believed that they could trust everything to God. They were not afraid to shake their fists in rage at the God of their creation, nor were they afraid to stomp their feet and shout for joy to Him! At all times they were willing to return to the One who had led them in the past. They believed in their ultimate deliverance. Here was their strength while waiting. Here was hope and a reason to go on, even as the "waters rose around their neck."

As Christians we too can go to this One, especially as we know him in Jesus. For here is the one who plunges into the water beside us. We are never alone. Thank God.

Prayer: As the waters rage and rise around us, O God, keep our eyes focused on the One who comes to us in the midst of all our pain. Let us not be too proud to ask for "Help!" from you, nor from the ones your Spirit sends to be our friends. Take our hand, precious Lord, and lead us home! Amen.

Handkerchiefs of God

All Saints Sunday

Scripture: Revelation 7:14b "Then he said to me, 'These are they who have come out of the great ordeal; they have washed their robes and made them white in the blood of the Lamb.'"

Today is All Saints Sunday. In many churches across the country this morning, the names of those who were members of the congregation and who have died since this day last year, will be read, and remembered, as a part of the worship service.

It is time for us again, to consider, what it means to be a saint of God.

In his book *Between the Dreaming and the Coming True* Robert Benson would say: "We do not always see the saints among us, but that is because we do not see what we are looking at. All the people in our lives are saints; it is just that some of them have day jobs, and most will never have feast days named for them."

And in his book called *Wishful Thinking* Frederick Beuchner writes: "In his holy flirtation with the world, God occasionally drops a handkerchief. Those handkerchiefs are called saints."

In a sermon that he preached on All Saints Sunday, just last year, Pastor Steven Loy began with the following thought:

"Today is the day we remember that we are all connected. We might like to believe that we are separate, that we are independent, but that is simply not the case. And what we remember today is that the people who have died continue to influence our lives. Those saints that we loved, the ones we couldn't stand, the ones that made us laugh and cry, and stop and think, are still among us even though we're not sure how."

Who were those people for you? We have a lot of people in our lives, someone mused, who are telling us what to do. When it comes to knowing how to live what we lack are not voices, but wise guides. Writes Clifton Guthrie, "What academic ethicists are rediscovering of course, is something that we have known already; that we are less influenced by abstract arguments than by the moral examples of other people—our mothers and fathers, our friends and neighbors, our oppressors and mentors."

Who are those people for you? Your mother? Your father? Your grandfather or grandmother? An aunt or an uncle, or a stranger who suddenly became your friend for no special reasons other than the sheer grace of it all?

On a day like today, I can't help but think about my Dad, who now rests from his labors. For those days that he willingly shared with me, in an age when it wasn't so normal for dads to spend much of their time with their children. He took the time. No matter how exhausted he may have been at the end of a busy day, he was never too tired to sit and read to me.

I remember our trips to the country—to uncle Art's farm—where dad grew up. He had been been parceled out there, by his widowed mother who simply couldn't take care of her six children nor find the food to feed them after my grandfather died at an early age.

I remember the old ramshackle barn where as a young boy Dad did the chores, as my uncle Art and aunt Elsie tried to eke out a living with about 15-20 dairy cows on less than 50 acres of hilly land. I remember milking cows myself, by hand—or trying.

I remember hunting for squirrels, harvesting hickory nuts and walnuts and butternuts that would one day be a part of Mom's wonderful cookies. Dad would teach me as we walked together. It was he who planted these seeds of wonder in me. It was Dad who helped me appreciate the beauty of God's created world; to understand what it really takes to farm the land. Those were the days that poetry started bubbling inside of me. It was my Dad who inspired me even though he would never claim to be a poet. He was truly, "one of God's handkerchiefs."

Uncle Art, aunt Elsie, Dad, his sister LaNore, who is a saint in my own mind just as surely as anyone is for me. She dedicated her life to the education of the Cree Indians in Northern Manitoba. She instilled in me a dream for adventure and a desire to push back the horizons of the world that I was given. There was my great grandpa from Norway, my Grandma from Czechoslovakia, and her prune klatches at Christmas time. All of them are gone now, but they are still there, inside of me.

It isn't our blood relatives alone that are in us. We inherit our "water relatives," too, the relatives with whom we are connected through Holy Baptism. Martin Luther, Martin Luther King Jr., Oscar Romero, Mother Teresa, Saint Francis, Teresa of Avila, and Joan of Arc, they are all in us in some way. They have nudged us to become more like the person we were created to be. They have reflected the love of Christ to us, and shaped us toward becoming a fuller human being.

We remember today, on All Saints Sunday, that even though these saints have died, we haven't lost them. We are still connected. Our relationship goes on in some way, for better or for worse.

Archbishop Romero started a practice in El Salvador that each Sunday at the Eucharist, the community would read the names of those who had died. After each name was read, the congregation would respond *Presente!* As we think of those names in our own mind and hearts today, as we remember them, we will certainly know and believe, that all those in Christ are still present today.

We pray today, in the words for our Prayer of the Day:

Prayer: Almighty God, whose people are knit together in one holy church, the body of Christ our Lord: Grant us grace to follow your blessed saints in lives of faith and commitment, and to know the inexpressible joys You have prepared for those who love You; through your Son, Jesus Christ our Lord, who lives and reigns with you and the Holy Spirit, one God, now and forever. Amen.

A Prayer for the Children

Scripture: Luke 18:17 "Truly I tell you, whoever does not receive the kingdom of God as a little child will never enter it."

One of the joys of having our grandchildren living so close is being able to share the little things with them. One of those moments happened on the day that my mother and dad celebrate their 60th Wedding Anniversary. I wrote a poem about it, and I share it with you now:

My Bee

"My bee sting me..." she sobbed
  "My bee sting me" and she
    Held her little "pinger"
      Out for all of us
        To see.

The bees were busy on that autumn afternoon,
  Taking all the sweetness
    From their world
      That they could
        Find.

"Emily" had captured one, "her bee", and she
  Kept it in a dish where she also
    Kept her caterpillar
      To touch, to look at
        And admire.

Her little "caperpillar" didn't seem to mind, nor
  Did her "progs" up north.
    Her little bee however
      Had other things
        In mind.

"My bee sting me" she wailed! Papa! Nama!
　　Anyone who would listen.
　　Wildly we ran, and sought
　　　To quickly soothe
　　　Her pain.

A little girl, a two year old, busy, and alive.
　　She was all about the task of touching
　　　Tasting, and discovering, the joys,
　　　And sorrows, of her
　　　Little world!

Children are such a joy! Or at least they should be. And
childhood should be such a wonderful time of their lives.
Unfortunately, that's not always true, and there are bigger
things than bee stings they must face. Marion Edelman would
call children, "the measure of our success." And in her book she
includes a powerful prayer for them:

We pray for children
　　Who sneak popsicles before supper
　　Who erase holes in math workbooks
　　Who can never find their shoes.
And we pray for those
　　Who stare at photographers from behind barbed wire,
　　Who can't bound down the street in a new pair of sneakers,
　　Who never "counted potatoes,"
　　Who are born in places we wouldn't be caught dead,
　　Who never go to the circus,
　　Who live in an X-rated world.
We pray for children who bring us sticky kisses, and fistfuls of
　　dandelions, who hug us in a hurry and forget their
　　lunch money.

And we pray for those
　　Who never get dessert,
　　Who have no safe blankets to drag behind them,
　　Who watch their parents watch them die,

Who can't find any bread to steal,
Who don't have any rooms to clean up,
Whose pictures aren't on anybody's dresser,
Whose monsters are real.

We pray for children,
Who spend all their allowance before Tuesday.
Who throw tantrums in the grocery store and pick at their
food.
Who like ghost stories.
Who shove dirty clothes under the bed, and never rinse out
the tub.
Who get visits from the tooth fairy,
Who don't like to be kissed in front of the carpool.
Who squirm in church or temple and scream in the phone,
Whose tears we sometimes laugh at and whose smiles can
make us cry.

And we pray for those
Who want to be carried
And for those who must,
For those we never give up on and for those
Who don't get a second chance.
For those we smother
And for those who will grab the hand
Of anybody kind enough to offer it.

(Please offer your hands to them, so that no child is left behind
because we did not act.)

**Prayer: Today, O Lord, we do pray for the children. Help us
to enjoy them, and to give them the space to wonder at the
world, the security and safety to live without fear. Help us to
learn from them, and to discover Your kingdom in the Hope in
their eyes. We pray in Jesus Name. Amen.**

Living Our Lives in Love

Scripture: John 14:12 "This is my commandment, that you love one another, as I have loved you."

Sometimes I come across things that almost seem too good to be true. It came across the "net," we say these days. I'm not even too sure who it is that tells the story, but at the top of the article, there were these letters, 'SHMILY'.

"My grandparents" the author writes, "were married for over half a century, and they played their own special game from the time that they had met each other. The goal of their game was to write the word "SHMILY" in a surprise place for the other to find.

They took turns leaving "SHMILY" around the house, and as soon as one of them discovered it, it was their turn to hide it once more. They dragged "SHMILY" with their fingers through the sugar and flour containers to await whoever was preparing the next meal. They smeared it in the dew on the windows overlooking the patio (where my grandma always fed us warm, homemade pudding with blue food coloring).

"SHMILY" was written in the steam left on the mirror after a hot shower where it would re-appear bath after bath. At one point, my grandmother even unrolled an entire roll of toilet paper to leave "SHMILY" on the very last sheet. There was no end to the places "SHMILY" would pop up.

Little notes with "SHMILY" scribbled hurriedly were found on dashboards and car seats, or taped to the steering wheel. The notes were stuffed inside shoes and left under pillows. "SHMILY" was written in the dust upon the mantel and traced in the ashes of the fireplace. This mysterious word was as much a part of my grandparents' house as the furniture. It took me a long time before I was able to fully appreciate my grandparents' game. Skepticism has kept me from believing in true love, one that is pure and enduring.

However, I never doubted my grandparents' relationship. They had love down pat. It was more than their flirtatious little games; it was a way of life. Their relationship was based on a devotion and passionate affection, which not everyone is lucky enough to experience. Grandma and Grandpa held hands every chance they could. They stole kisses as they bumped into each other in their tiny kitchen. They finished each other's sentences and shared the daily crossword puzzle and word jumble. My grandma whispered to me about how cute my grandpa was, and how handsome he had grown to be. She claimed that she really knew "how to pick 'em." Before every meal they bowed their heads and gave thanks, marveling at their blessings; a wonderful family, good fortune and each other.

But there was a dark cloud in my grandparent's lives. My grandmother had breast cancer. The disease had first appeared ten years earlier.

As always, Grandpa was with her every step of the way. He comforted her in their yellow room, painted that way so that she could always be surrounded by sunshine, even when she was too sick to go outside. Now the cancer was again attacking her body. With the help of a cane and my grandfather's steady hand, they went to church, every morning. But, my grandmother grew steadily weaker, until finally she could not leave the house anymore. For a while Grandpa would go to church alone, praying to God to watch over his wife. Then one day what we all dreaded finally happened. Grandma was gone.

"SHMILY". It was scrawled in yellow on the pink ribbons of my grandmother's funeral bouquet. As the crowd thinned and the last mourners turned to leave, my aunts, uncles, cousins and other family members came forward and gathered around Grandma one last time.

Grandpa stepped up to my grandmother's casket and taking a shaky breath, he began to sing to her. Through his tears and grief, the song came (a deep throaty lullaby).

Shaking with my own sorrow, I will never forget that moment. For I knew that although I couldn't begin to fathom the depth of their love, I had been privileged to witness its unmatched beauty.

"S-H-M-I-L-Y" See how much I love you.

Thank you, Grandma and Grandpa, for letting me see."

As I said before, I'm not sure where this little story came from. But I like to believe, it's true.

Prayer: O Lord, for those who have modeled the depth of love in our lives, we give you thanks today. Allow us the grace to let that same love live in us. That we may discover its power, its strength, and its hope in our lives, we pray today. For the Love that you have given us O Lord, in the person of your son, who went to the depths for us because of His love, we give you thanks and praise. In Jesus Name. Amen.

Come to Me

Scripture: Matthew 11:28-29 "Come to me, all you who are weary and are carrying heavy burdens, and I will give you rest. Take my yoke upon you, and learn from me, for I am humble in heart, and you will find rest for your souls."

Jesus issues an invitation to us today. "Come to me," He says. "And I will give you rest."

Could this be the same Jesus who but a week earlier in our Gospel lesson challenged us to a Cross? Could this be the same Jesus who served us fair warning that to follow him would mean conflict and division within our human families? Or that if we wished to find our lives we would first have to lose them? Could this be the same Jesus that said he had not come to bring peace into the world, but a sword? There is a cost to our discipleship, he told us then, and the cost would mean deep personal sacrifice, and pain, perhaps even the loss of our lives.

His words for us today are soft and inviting, not hard and demanding. "Take my yoke upon you" he says, "and learn from me. For I am gentle and humble in heart, and you will find rest for your souls."

Once again we enter the paradox of this Gospel message. We need to hear both messages, and both are important for us to hear. Throughout this unusual New Testament story of Jesus and his church, time and again we will see that the Gospel is challenging as well as comforting, tumultuous as well as peaceful, stimulating as well as soothing, judgmental as well as accepting, complex yet simple, exhausting yet restful, rugged yet gentle, personal as well as communal.

So I encourage you to let his word of Comfort come into your life today.

His message comes to those who are exhausted. He speaks to those who have looked everywhere in their search for the truth. He speaks to those who are looking for good in their lives, and offers them a way. It is His Way.

It was St. Augustine who prayed, "You have made us for yourself, O Christ, and our hearts are restless, until they find their rest in You."

"Come to me" says Jesus. "If you have suffered indignity and humiliation; if you have felt rejected and unloved, come to me".

"If you have been a victim, come to me."

"If an illness has suddenly come into your life and you're scared to death, come to me."

"If death has suddenly interrupted everything you are and have been doing, come to me."

Jesus enters the poverty of our lives today, if we will accept his invitation.

When was the last time you stepped outside in the summer darkness and looked at the night sky? Have the stars lost their twinkle for you? How is it that our eyes fail to follow the line of green trees to the stretches of the sky? How little our perspective becomes sometimes! Here before the uncluttered sky, we are invited to see again the wonder and beauty of silver dotted space and quiet majesty.

So often our eyes look only to ourselves for the answers to our questions. But Jesus wants us to know that with Him there is a presence and peace if we can hear his gentle whispering. Here there is a yoke that is easy, and a burden that is light. There is a person, in the midst of the vastness, who enters our weariness and offers us rest for our souls.

Prayer: Life gets weary, sometimes, O Lord. Our lives ache with the weariness, and our souls are parched with need, a thirst that no one can assuage. Help us to listen carefully to your gentle invitation, and to know that You are there. In Jesus Name. Amen.

Some Singers Needed

Scripture: Psalm 149:1 "Praise the Lord! Sing to the Lord a new song, his praise in the assembly of the faithful."

This morning I'm listening to the cardinal's song. The windows and the doors are closed, but still the cardinal's song is able to break my reverie, come into my home, into my heart.

Beyond the pond the tall grass waves in the morning wind. Outside my door the flowers bloom. Just as they were meant to do.

The morning paper didn't say a thing about the tall grass waving in the wind. In all its pages there was nary a picture of a flower in bloom. Nor was there any mention of the beauty of the birdsong.

"Three killed in a Crystal shooting," the headlines screamed. "J.R. Rider arrested for possession of marijuana." "19 dead from a blast in Saudi Arabia."

And so it goes, each day, in the daily news.

Two completely different pictures of life are swirling around my head today. Which do I listen to? Do I plug my ears to one in favor of another? How hard it would be to heal, be whole, I thought, if we listened only to the daily news.

In a little book called, *I'm Thinking of You* Herb Brokering writes:

"I'm sending you verbs today: Sing. Bloom."

Singing is what birds do because of who they are. But not every bird song is a pretty song. The grackles and the crows would never try out for the Bird Barbershop Quartet.

Yet still they sing.

And flowers bloom. That's just what flowers do. The tall grass waves in the morning wind.

Ours is the choice. We cannot ignore the realities of a world that swirls around us with death, nor do we dare close our eyes to the anguish of the world.

But the world needs some singers here. Some bloomers. Some folks who are willing to dance in the morning wind. An aching world needs some healing. So I'm sending you verbs today: Sing! Bloom! Dance!

Prayer: You're listening this morning, aren't you, Lord? You want to hear a new song. Grackles, crows, cardinals, and bluebirds...make us members, O God, of the Bird Barbershop Quartet! In Jesus Name. Amen.

I Wish You Enough

Scripture: 2 Thessalonians 2:15 "So then, brothers and sister, stand firm and hold fast to the traditions that you were taught by us, either by word of mouth or by letter."

In St. Paul's second letter to the Thessalonians, he cautions people "not to be quickly shaken in mind or alarmed" about the coming of the Lord Jesus, "to the effect that the day of the Lord is already here." (2 Thessalonians 2:1-2)

There appeared to have been many in that little Christian church who were convinced that they were in the midst of the beginning of the end. St. Paul seeks to calm their fears. He urges them in the midst of the changes and challenges that surround them, especially in the face of those who persecute them, not only to be calm, but "to stand firm and hold fast to the traditions" that they were taught.

Since September 11, 2001, there are many in our day who have also been alarmed and quickly shaken.

One of our major radio stations here in the Twin Cities recently interviewed the authors of the popular "Left Behind" series of novels. These books are based on the premise that the "Day of the Lord" is already here, and that we are but a heart-beat away from the end of the world.

I think it's time to look for another perspective. It makes me angry when people play on our fears in a ploy to market their books. It also makes me angry when journalists and media personalities insensitively escalate our fears by airing such things. I think there are far too many talk shows on the radio and on television these days, and they do little to bring us closer to the truth we need to hear.

I would urge all of us to step away from radio and television, and to seek a new perspective. We need to hear the calming and the reassuring voices of the Bible in the midst of crises like these.

Those same assurances that we hear in St. Paul's letter today can be heard in the Psalmists prayer as well. "I call upon you and you will answer me God; incline your ear to me, and hear my words. Wondrously show your steadfast love, O Savior of those who seek refuge. Guard me as the apple of the eye; hide me in the shadow of Your wings, from the wicked who despoil me, my deadly enemies who surround me." (Psalm 17:6-8)

Sometimes I hear that we are our own worst enemies.

Not long ago someone shared with me this little thought. It's simply called, "Enough."

Recently I overheard a father and a daughter in their last moments together. They had announced her departure and standing near the security gate, they hugged, and he said, "I love you. I wish you enough." She in turn said, "Daddy, our life together has been more than enough. Your love is all I ever needed. I wish you enough, too, Daddy."

They kissed and she left. He walked over toward the window where I was seated. Standing there, I could see he wanted and needed to cry. I tried not to intrude on his privacy, but he welcomed me in by asking, "Did you ever say goodbye to someone, knowing it would be forever?"

"Yes, I have," I replied. Saying that brought back memories I had of expressing my love and appreciation for all my Dad had done for me. Recognizing that his days were limited, I took the time to tell him face to face how much he meant to me. So I knew what this man was experiencing.

"Forgive me for asking, but why is this a forever goodbye?" I asked.

"I am old, and she lives much too far away. I have challenges ahead, and the reality is, the next trip back would be for my funeral," he said.

"When you were saying goodbye, I heard you say, 'I wish you enough'. May I ask what that means?"

He began to smile. "That's a wish that has been handed down from other generations. My parents used to say it to everyone." He paused for a moment, and looking up as if trying to remember it in detail, he smiled even more.

"When we said, 'I wish you enough', we were wanting the other person to have a life filled with just enough good things to sustain them," he continued, and then turning toward me he shared the following as if he were reciting it from memory.

I wish you enough sun to keep your attitude bright.

I wish you enough rain to appreciate the sun more.

I wish you enough happiness to keep your spirit alive.

I wish you enough pain so that the smallest joys in life appear much bigger.

I wish you enough gain to satisfy your wanting.

I wish you enough loss to appreciate all that you possess.

I wish you enough "Hellos" to get you through the final "Goodbye."

He then began to sob and walked away. (Author unknown)

" Stand firm and hold fast," St. Paul would urge us, "to the traditions that you were taught." God has given us just "enough" grace in the Cross of Jesus Christ. And so, fellow travelers, I wish you "enough" faith to see and know that grace, that you may be sustained in your fears and not be alarmed. May you know that you are the apple of God's eye, and may you rest in the shelter of his wings."

Prayer: We call upon you, O Lord, once more, for clarity of vision and the strength of a new perspective. Give us enough of those things that sustain us and keep our spirits alive, so that we are not lost in our fears. We pray today, for just enough trust in You, not to be lost in ourselves. In Jesus Name. Amen.

Acknowledgments

Grateful acknowledgment is made to the following authors, agents, publishers and other copyright holders for the use of material quoted in this book. Every effort has been made to locate all copyright holders. If any material has been used without proper credit, please notify the author so that proper credit can be given in future editions.

From *Wheels in the Air* by William Joyner. Copyright 1968 by Pilgrim Press.

From *Stories for the Journey* by William White. Copyright 1988. Reprinted by permission of the publisher, Augsburg Fortress, Mpls., MN.

From *The Longest Advent* by the Rev. Becca Stevens. First published in *Alive Now* by Upper Room Publishers, December 1998, used with permission of the author.

From *The Way of the Wolf* by Martin Bell. 1968. Excerpted from permission

"Whoever Finds This" reprinted from *A Third Helping of Chicken Soup for the Soul*, Health Communications, Inc. Deerfield Beach. Author unknown.

"God in the Park" from *Advent, Christmas, and Epiphany* by Megan McKenna, Copyright 1998, Used with permission of the publisher, Orbis Book, Maryknoll, New York.

From *Stories for the Journey* by William White, Copyright 1988. Reprinted by permission of the publisher, Augsburg-Fortress, Mpls., Mn.

From *Disturbed by Joy*, sermons of Edmund Steimle, Copyright 1967. Fortress Press. Excerpted from permission.

From *Gospel of John (2)* by William Barclay. Copyright 1955. Reprinted by permission of the publisher, Westminster John Knox Press, Louisville, KY.

From *Who Speaks for God* by Jim Wallis, Copyright 1996. Reprinted by permission of the publisher, Delacorte Press, Bantam Doubleday Dell Publishing Group, Inc., New York, and N.Y.

From *Teaching Your Children About God*, by David Wolpe, Copyright 1993 by David Wolpe. Reprinted by permission of Henry Holt and Co., LLC